Modern Ireland: A Very Short Introduction

VERY SHORT INTRODUCTIONS are for anyone wanting a stimulating and accessible way into a new subject. They are written by experts, and have been translated into more than 45 different languages.

The series began in 1995, and now covers a wide variety of topics in every discipline. The VSI library now contains over 500 volumes—a Very Short Introduction to everything from Psychology and Philosophy of Science to American History and Relativity—and continues to grow in every subject area.

Titles in the series include the following:

Senia Pašeta

MODERN IRELAND

A Very Short Introduction

OXFORD
UNIVERSITY PRESS

Great Clarendon Street, Oxford OX2 6DP

Oxford University Press is a department of the University of Oxford.
It furthers the University's objective of excellence in research, scholarship,
and education by publishing worldwide in

Oxford New York

Auckland Cape Town Dar es Salaam Hong Kong Karachi
Kuala Lumpur Madrid Melbourne Mexico City Nairobi
New Delhi Shanghai Taipei Toronto

With offices in
Argentina Austria Brazil Chile Czech Republic France Greece
Guatemala Hungary Italy Japan Poland Portugal Singapore
South Korea Switzerland Thailand Turkey Ukraine Vietnam

Oxford is a registered trade mark of Oxford University Press
in the UK and in certain other countries

First published as a Very Short Introduction 2003

British Library Cataloguing in Publication Data

Data available

Library of Congress Cataloging in Publication Data

Paseta, Senia
Modern Ireland: a very short introduction / Senia Paseta

p. cm
Includes bibliographical references (p.) and index

1. Ireland-History-19th Century. 2. Ireland-History-20th Century.
3. Ireland Civilization. I. Title. II. Series.
DA950.P37 2003
941.508–dc21   2002193105

ISBN 978-0-19-280167-8

20

Typeset by RefineCatch, Bungay, Suffolk
Printed in Great Britain by
Ashford Colour Press Ltd., Gosport, Hampshire.

For Simon

Contents

Preface

A book of this size cannot hope to masquerade as total history, and readers must understand that the choice of subject matter will necessarily reveal the biases and interests of the writer. This book is not aimed at the initiated, and I hope it will be accessible to people with little or no knowledge of modern Irish history. Each chapter deals with a particular period of modern Irish history, though themes and developments cross the years and the decades. Because of the brevity of this book, selecting a hierarchy of events and individuals for inclusion was a difficult task. The focus is broadly political, and I am sorry not to have been able to include more discussion of the lived realities of Irish and Northern Irish life. I hope that this very brief sketch will whet appetites for further reading.

I owe a great debt to a number of generous friends and colleagues who contributed in more ways than they know to the writing of this book. Shelley Cox and Rebecca O'Connor were exemplary editors and co-conspirators. Philip Bull, Roy Foster, Neal Garnham, Selina Guinness, Marc Mulholland, John Robertson, and Charles Townshend listened patiently to my often disjointed thoughts and offered incisive comments on draft chapters. Many thanks too to my students, who told me what they would like to see in a book of this kind. As always, I am deeply grateful to Katarina Pašeta for unswerving loyalty, and to Simon Riley for his astute suggestions and for the unwavering confidence he displayed in this book and its author – despite disagreeing with both at times.

SP
Oxford 2002

List of illustrations

The publisher and the author apologize for any errors or omissions in the above list. If contacted they will be pleased to rectify these at the earliest opportunity.

Modern Ireland: Towns, Counties, and Provinces.

Chapter 1
The Act of Union

The Act of Union between Great Britain and Ireland which came into effect on 1 January 1801 presents historians with a convenient but far from straightforward starting point for a survey of modern Irish history. Many of the conflicts that have characterized Irish political, social, and economic life since 1800 were in place well before the Act was introduced. International events were already exacerbating local tensions. The violent and dynamic final three decades of the 18th century which prompted the introduction of the Act were themselves products of a longer and constantly evolving struggle between competing political minds, identities, and programmes. The Act of Union attempted to address the issues underlying the conflicts, but, as we shall see, each one continued to simmer throughout the next two centuries.

Land and population

Ireland in the 18th century was an overwhelmingly rural society whose strong regional variations nurtured a diversity of political, social, and economic cultures. Visitors to the country generally agreed that by British standards, Irish farming practices were backward. On the other hand, some pronounced themselves surprised by the existence of forward-thinking landlords and industrialists in Ireland. Standards, customs, and agricultural practices varied greatly across the country, depending on natural conditions and patterns of land ownership and management. Famine was recurrent and was usually caused by bad weather or crop failure. Two particularly severe instances in 1728–9 and 1740–1, and the attendant spread of diseases including typhus and dysentery, caused enormous suffering.

As in all European countries in the 18th century, the social order reflected the importance of land ownership. At the top of the social and political hierarchy were landlords. They were followed by tenant farmers to whom they leased land, and the cottiers who usually rented land on a year-by-year basis and were the most susceptible to economic downturns. The expansion of trade and industry also facilitated the development of new social hierarchies. Economic advantage was more sharply contested than ever before as growing numbers of middle-class Catholic and Presbyterian merchants, professionals, and industrialists showed that wealth could be attained from sources other than the land.

Religion

Ireland's population had increased rapidly from about 2.5 million in 1767 to over 4 million by 1781. It was to reach 5 million by 1800, and over 7.5 million in 1831. The not altogether reliable religious census of 1834 estimated that almost 81% of the population was Catholic, 10.7% was Anglican, and 9% was Presbyterian; 99% of the country's Presbyterians and 45% of its Anglicans lived in Ulster. Anglicans also had a strong presence in and around Dublin, but were otherwise scattered throughout the east and west. The most important point to be drawn from these statistics is that numerically speaking, Anglicans and Presbyterians were strongest in the same area. This would have important consequences for their increasing cooperation in the face of what were perceived to be Catholic threats to the Protestant constitution.

About 5,000 Protestant families owned 95% of Irish land. Owing its privileged position to the conquest of Gaelic Ireland from the

16th century, this elite came to be collectively known as the Protestant Ascendancy. It was (often loosely and inaccurately) defined by its religion, its ownership of property, its adherence to notions of traditional privilege, and by social conventions. The Ascendancy dominated politics, the civil service, and high society, but it was far more fluid and variable than this simple template would suggest. Throughout the 18th century, while land ownership conferred status, it did not necessarily confer wealth. And, just as impecunious landlords were not uncommon, neither were ambitious and successful professionals. This was particularly true of lawyers, who cut a swathe through high society and gained political clout in the Irish parliament.

The incontrovertible identifying feature of this elite was Anglicanism. This distinguished them in crucial ways from Catholics and from other Irish Protestants. Presbyterians were excluded from this hierarchy, but throughout the 18th century they expanded their own economic and political influence. Most Presbyterians were tenant farmers and merchants, their concentration in the north of Ireland allowing them favourable access to trade and industrial sectors and to relative security of tenure. They maintained strong ties with Scotland and through their kirk sessions exercised real jurisdiction in local communities.

The forced payment of tithes to the Church of Ireland and their exclusion from public office until 1780 aroused bitter resentment among Presbyterians, especially in the face of what they perceived to be their proven loyalty to the Protestant constitution. Most legal constraints were removed by the end of the century, but they left a legacy of mistrust.

The Catholic question will be dealt with in more detail in the next chapter, but a few preliminaries should be sketched before we proceed. Though suspicion of Irish Catholics was already rife, they came under increasing scrutiny in the aftermath of the Williamite War of 1689–91, during which many Catholics joined James II in his campaign against the Protestant William III. A number of the battles fought during this conflict came to occupy an important place in Protestant culture and memory, while helping to reinforce notions of Catholic untrustworthiness and treachery. Having fought on the losing side, Catholics were subjected to a series of laws that aimed to fortify the Protestant dominance of Irish society.

Early examples of these penal (or no popery) laws included banning Catholics from carrying weapons and forbidding them from teaching or managing Irish schools or travelling to the Continent to be educated. A 1704 act made land ownership extremely difficult by prohibiting Catholics from taking up leases for longer than 31 years and from inheriting land from Protestants. As land ownership was in any case the privilege of a tiny minority, few Catholics were actually dispossessed under this legislation. Similarly, though few Catholics (and Protestants) had been eligible to vote, those who had were completely disenfranchised by 1728.

As memories of 17th-century Catholic insurgence began to fade, toleration seemed to increase. The penal laws began to be dismantled. Relief acts in 1778 and 1782 loosened the restrictions on Catholic land ownership, education, and participation in the professions, but a number of restraints remained, ensuring that Catholic grievances formed a crucial part in wider political debates and controversies.

The Irish administration

Ireland in the 18th century was a kingdom with its own legislature and officials, but its autonomy was undermined by its dependence on Great Britain, the senior partner in the constitutional relationship between the islands. Domestic political power was centred on the Irish parliament in Dublin's College Green. Landlords were strongly represented, but lawyers, other professionals, and merchants were also elected. It was of course unrepresentative of the wider Irish population – especially the

Catholic portion of it – but this was not a democratic age and the existence in Ireland of rotten boroughs and irregular electoral practices hardly marked it out as unique. The Irish parliament's lineage stretched back to the Middle Ages, but its independence and composition had varied greatly throughout the centuries. Until 1782, the 18th-century body had restricted powers and was ultimately subservient to Westminster.

The application to Ireland of the colonial label is problematic as the shared experiences of religious and political upheaval ensured that the two countries were more closely linked than was usual with British dependencies. Moreover, the close proximity of the countries and Ireland's susceptibility to attack from Britain's continental enemies guaranteed that ties between them would remain strong. The Irish administration became more elaborate and bulky as the century progressed, and the relationship between the native parliament and British officials increasingly turned on the question of the limits of Irish autonomy.

The Irish parliament signified the separateness of Ireland from the United Kingdom, but the Irish executive indicated its subordination. The executive was appointed by and responsible to London. It was based at Dublin Castle, and presided over by the Irish Viceroy or Lord Lieutenant. 'Dublin Castle' or the 'Castle' became shorthand (and usually derisory) terms for the British administration in Ireland. The Viceroyalty evolved into a largely ceremonial position. The Lord Lieutenant was aided by the Chief Secretary, a member of the House of Commons who supervised Castle administration and oversaw the implementation of Irish policy.

Government policy was upheld by a legal and judicial system which, though unique in some ways, was strongly based on an English model. The government appointed all officers of the law, the vast majority of whom were Anglicans. Patronage was a fact of Castle life and yet another source of bitter complaint for Irish Catholics. They

1. *The Irish House of Commons* (1870), by Francis Wheatley, features Grattan espousing enhanced legislative powers for the Irish parliament.

were largely excluded from the civil service, judiciary, and higher positions in the police force of the country. Order was upheld in part by a strong garrison presence, whose numbers fluctuated in line with conditions in the country. Locally recruited troops, along with the regular army, were frequently deployed in support of the civil power.

Agrarian politics

As pressure for land increased in line with population growth, so too did agrarian violence. Signs of major local discontent could be seen in parts of the country decades before the outbreak of rebellion in 1798. Such movements aimed primarily to address specific grievances. Issues that aroused dissatisfaction included rents, tithes, evictions, and wages, and protest could be aimed at landlords, clergy, and even tenant farmers who sub-let to cottiers and agricultural labourers. Protest tactics ranged from threatening letters to the maiming of animals and destruction of property and life. Agrarian 'secret societies' adopted names that befitted their clandestine character, the most famous including the Rightboys, Hearts of Oak, and the Whiteboys.

Such societies were manifestly neither national nor nationalist, but they did contain within them the potential for a broader form of political organization. Agrarian agitation was worst during periods of economic instability. Protest was often traditionalist rather than politically radical, and was usually targeted at innovation and interruptions to what were perceived to be traditional forms of rural life. Agrarian secret societies became more and more sectarian as the century progressed, reflecting both deep and ancient suspicions between religious communities and contemporary political and economic realities. More explicit confessional identification became evident in areas where Catholics and Protestants were likely to live in close proximity and be competing for work, land, and resources. The densely populated County Armagh became a particular focus of a number of celebrated showdowns which were driven by a combination of anxieties, including the employment of Catholics in linen weaving in the county and competition for land.

Defenderism emerged in the 1780s and within a decade its politics had spread east and west and as far as Dublin. Its expansion was intimately linked to contemporary economic factors and to what appeared to be a slackening of deference and increasing Catholic assurance in the face of relaxation and non-enforcement of penal laws. Like other rural protest groups, it objected to tithes, taxation, and high rents on potato plots, but its explicitly local economic campaigns were but one aspect of a political movement whose aims and methods were constantly evolving and becoming more radical and ambitious.

Recent scholarship has noted its organization along Masonic lines and its recourse to secret signs, symbols, and oaths. This was not unknown, but the language and symbolism of the Defenders betrayed a more sophisticated and ideological bent than most of its counterparts. This was to make it more susceptible to involvement in broader political trends at national and international levels, and some Defenders were certainly keen followers and supporters of revolutionary events in France. Moreover, the organization appeared to have won some support in towns and among sections of the non-agrarian population.

But at the heart of the movement was sectarianism: as its name implies, this was an organization that aimed to defend Catholics. Some scholars have argued that the very sectarianism of the Defenders diminished as it spread from its original base in Armagh into neighbouring counties and beyond. There is good evidence for this, and the alliance formed between the Defenders and the United Irishmen supports the notion that confessional divisions could sometimes be overcome in the interests of larger causes.

But this must not be exaggerated. The Defenders grew and developed amidst rising sectarian tensions, particularly in Ulster, and they were the perpetrators and victims of plainly sectarian raids, public clashes, and riots. One of the most famous was the Battle of the Diamond, a clash in 1795 between the Defenders and the Protestant Peep O'Day Boys near the village of Loughgall in County Armagh. The victorious Peep O'Day Boys reorganized themselves in the aftermath of the battle as the Orange Order, the name being adopted in honour of King William III and his victory at the Boyne in 1690. The fact that it was thought necessary to organize Protestants along more rigid lines reflects mounting concern about what were perceived to be Catholic advances and their corollary, the undermining of Protestant power and privilege.

The Order established grand lodges in Ulster and Dublin in 1797. Its gradual development from local roots into a national organization reflected heightened political tension and violence in the 1790s, particularly in Ulster. Rumours about schemes to eliminate Protestants and Catholics spread through already anxious communities. And although some parts of the country experienced this period as relatively peaceful, talk of coups, massacres, and plots became commonplace in some circles. This was clearly a time of mounting tension, and it is in the context of such swelling economic, political, and religious pressures that we can begin to better understand the course of Irish politics in this period. Questions of religious identity were to remain at the heart of each of the developments that would lead before the turn of the 19th century to armed rebellion.

Constitutional politics

The exclusively Protestant Irish parliament was far removed from the shadowy world of agrarian violence, but it was not immune from its consequences. It was in many ways a replica of the British parliament, and, like Westminster, it was alive with political intrigue and controversy throughout the century. One of the main themes around which political debate raged in the 18th century was the question of how much independence from Westminster the

Dublin legislature did and should have. The concept of Patriotism evolved during the second half of the century, attracting men with varied interests to its ranks. At a basic level, this was a form of colonial or proto-nationalism which emphasized the view that Ireland suffered through its subservience to the British legislature.

Some Patriots highlighted economic grievances, others the rights of Protestants in the face of the relaxation of penal laws and the tendency of Catholics to seek redress from London, while others still demanded greater legislative independence. The patriot group in the Irish parliament did not seem to make much headway and faced indifference if not outright opposition. Events in College Green were deeply dependent on and influenced by English politics, but it was an international crisis which was to give the patriots a much needed shot in the arm. The American Revolution had an important impact on Irish politics, not only because the English became increasingly distracted by events across the Atlantic, but also because various groups of Irishmen could find parallels in the American situation for their own.

The American Revolution induced economic distress through restrictions on trade with America and a squeezing of British expenditure to pay for the war. It also brought about instability as numbers of British troops were removed from Ireland and fears of a French invasion mounted. The government's response to such concern about security was to establish Volunteer companies across Ireland which prepared to undertake military and law-enforcement duties until the crisis passed. Despite the penal laws Catholics were permitted to join these Volunteer corps from an early stage. The involvement of Catholics in the defence of Ireland was, however, too much for some Protestants to bear. Some local corps refused to admit Catholics, while others accepted them only very grudgingly.

The Volunteers created problems for the administration because, despite their commitment to the defence of Ireland, they were not necessarily loyal to the government. Moreover, it was a large force with the potential to adopt an ethos at odds with authority. Attempts to turn the force into a legal and regular militia failed. In fact, despite the opposition of some Volunteers, the organization became increasingly sympathetic to the patriots and to notions of greater legislative independence for Ireland. This was fostered by the involvement in the Volunteers of well-known patriots, including Henry Grattan who helped to direct the movement down a reformist path. Volunteering played an important role in Ireland, not least because it allowed Irishmen from the middle and upper middle classes to play an active role in national affairs during a volatile time. The key word here is national. Their focus was Ireland and their duty was to protect it. Coupled with the spectacle of the forces of the Crown being humiliated by American upstarts, Volunteering encouraged notions of active citizenship and, increasingly, of a broader patriotism.

Parliamentary reform

The Volunteers were eventually broadened, radicalized, and politicized. This was particularly the case for Ulster corps, 143 of which declared their explicit support for Irish legislative independence in 1782. Support for this campaign also gathered momentum in the Dublin parliament. In 1782 legislative amendments granted Ireland a number of concessions, including parliamentary independence, limited money bills, and the independence of judges. As always in matters of Irish parliamentary politics, shifting allegiances and power blocs at Westminster had played a major role in the passing of this legislation.

The questions of what this parliament actually did and whom it in fact represented raise difficulties. In the first instance, the Irish parliament did not acquire full independence. Though it was used very rarely, the English Privy Council still had the power to veto Irish bills and British politicians continued to preside over the Irish executive. But the biggest question facing the Irish parliament was the issue of Catholic reform.

One of the outcomes of the Irish parliament's reluctance to grant Catholic emancipation was that Irish Catholics tended to look to London for redress of grievances, rather than to Dublin. This of course exposed them to accusations of disloyalty to the Dublin parliament, but it had become clear very quickly that the 'independent' Irish parliament was no more open to Catholic relief than its predecessor had been. Irish parliamentary attitudes towards Catholics were thus out of step with cosmopolitan thinking.

Though Catholics had prominent Irish supporters in the Irish parliament, it was largely British pressure that forced a reluctant Irish parliament to accept a bill in 1793 to enfranchise the Catholics who met a property qualification of 40 shillings. Catholics were still excluded from actually sitting in parliament. However, the ungenerous and grudging way in which these concessions had been wrung from the Dublin parliament only served to encourage the radicalization of politically minded Catholics.

The United Irishmen

Synonymous with the revolutionary events of the 1790s was the Society of United Irishmen, originally a constitutional organization founded in 1791, first in Belfast and a month later in Dublin. It drew support mainly from Protestants, especially in Belfast, though Catholics joined the Dublin chapter in increasing numbers. Aims included the extension of parliamentary reform, the end of corruption in politics, Catholic relief, and the further loosening of English influence in Irish affairs. Elements contained within it included libertarianism, republicanism, dissenting traditions, Catholic emancipationism, patriotism, and Whig doctrine. But beyond this – and even these aims assumed varied complexions in different branches of the Society – what bound this organization?

The name United Irishmen points to the aspirations of some of its founders, but these were largely to be disappointed, as this organization too was to succumb to sectarian fracturing. While there is no doubt that the Society was inspired by the French Revolution, individual members drew their own lessons from events in France. Some revelled in its republicanism, others in its egalitarian rhetoric. But such sentiment was not automatically compatible with religious pluralism. A distrust of Catholics was retained by the many radically inclined Presbyterians who joined the Society, particularly in Belfast. In some minds, republicanism could easily be combined with the virtues of exclusionist Protestantism, and the French Revolution could itself be celebrated as a victory against the infidel Catholic Church.

The subject of the transformation of the United Irishmen from a constitutional to a revolutionary society is a fascinating but complex one. The reasons for this change must be seen in the context of events in France, of course, but also in light of rising British panic about radical political activity in Ireland and in Britain. Underlying this was a fear of French intervention in Irish affairs. The government's response was a series of laws which aimed to curb such activity. This, coupled with a lack of parliamentary reform, encouraged the radicalization of the Society, which re-emerged in 1795, following its suppression in the previous year, as a secret, republican, and revolutionary organization. A core of such advanced opinion had existed in the organization before its proscription, but government repression gave it the spur it needed. Over the next four years it was restructured as a more discplined and militarily inclined organization.

Links between the United Irishmen and other societies were increasingly established. Co-founder and prominent United Irishman Wolf Tone had become president of the progressive Catholic Committee in 1792, encouraging Catholic involvement in the United Irishmen. Severely curtailed in 1793, radically minded Volunteers also drifted towards the United Irishmen in the early 1790s. Enthused by the French Revolution – often because it was seen as a Catholic triumph – Defenders also joined, and by 1796 a more formal link between the two organizations had been forged. In some areas, boundaries between the two organizations were in fact very fluid. In addition to this, Tone and his allies had been cultivating links with French supporters in the hope of gaining military support for an Irish republic. They had some success and a French expedition set sail for Ireland in late 1796. It turned back because of poor weather, but news of the aborted expedition sent waves of alarm through the already apprehensive Westminster and Castle administrations.

The 1798 Rising

United Irish attempts to stage a revolution were hampered by a number of factors, including government repression and espionage, dissension within the movement itself, and disorganization. Tone had gone into exile in 1795, first to America and then to France. Ireland, meanwhile, was descending into further disorder. The authorities clamped down on seditious behaviour. Large numbers of suspected insurgents were imprisoned, weapons searches were undertaken, and martial law was finally declared in March 1798. A government yeomanry corps had also been raised in 1796. Protestants dominated this force, which displayed an anti-Catholic character and close links with the Orange Order.

Radicals themselves were faced with a sharp choice given the infiltration of their organizations and the exile and arrest of some leaders. A rebellion might fail, but delaying while the organization experienced further deterioration in fact guaranteed defeat. The National Directory took the decision to rise, but the ensuing rebellion is better described as a series of local battles than a national campaign, though the scale of violence was huge. Around 50,000 rebels were involved in the uprising. The four main centres of violence were central Leinster, eastern Ulster, County Wexford, and Connacht, the latter largely as a response to a French landing at Killala Bay, County Mayo, in late August.

These battles were short-lived but bloody and, in Wexford in particular, naked sectarianism was in evidence. About 30,000 people had been killed by the end of the summer. Tone was himself sentenced to death after his arrest off the Irish coast; subsequently he committed suicide in a last dramatic gesture. Even after the last of the sporadic fighting had been suppressed, informal retribution and government retaliation against the insurgents continued. About 150,000 people were subjected to flogging, transportation, or execution, though a number of sentences were commuted as post-rebellion panic died down.

The Rising was a traumatic episode whose impact on the subsequent history of Ireland was acute. Allegiances had shifted rapidly during the crisis, not least because secular and republican aspirations could not in the end overcome older and ultimately more compelling confessional identities and suspicions. As many historians have emphasized, the rebellion to unite all Irishmen in fact exacerbated divisions rather than removing them.

The Act of Union

Plans for union between Great Britain and Ireland had been mooted well before 1798, but the extraordinary conditions of the late 18th century provided a powerful context for their implementation. In the mind of Pitt a union offered two main attractions: a mechanism for bringing Ireland more firmly under the control of Britain, and the chance to push through Catholic emancipation. He hoped that the latter would help to quell dissent and to nurture a loyal Catholic population within the context of the United Kingdom. In the end it did nothing of the kind, as strong opposition compelled Pitt to leave aside plans for Catholic emancipation. This was a grave error whose consequences were far-reaching.

Plans for Union were denounced by a number of blocs, most vocally by 'patriots', the Orange Order, and a variety of professional and business interests. Most Catholics were won over, especially as they believed that Catholic emancipation would follow. After a period of intense debate, the legislation was shepherded through the parliaments by a determined British administration. Many commentators denounced Irish parliamentarians for succumbing to English flattery and bribery. Some Irish MPs were indeed 'rewarded' for their backing of the legislation, but while this corruption was perhaps more extensive than was usual, the granting of favours in exchange for political support was hardly unique in the close world of 18th-century politics; neither were such tactics unique to the unionist camp. The motion was carried by both houses in March 1800 and received the Royal Assent in August.

Demands for the repeal and reform of the Union and strenuous resistance to its removal underpinned nationalism and unionism in modern Ireland. The most important aspect of the Act was the abolition of the Irish parliament and the transfer of Irish representation to the united parliament at Westminster. There were to be 100 Irish MPs in the House of Commons (64 county seats, 35 borough seats, and one for Dublin University), and 28 temporal lords and four Church of Ireland bishops in the House of Lords. In terms of raw population statistics Ireland was to be under-represented at Westminster (though this had changed by the end of the 19th century due to rapid population decline).

The Act also specified new financial arrangements between Ireland and Great Britain. It allowed for the abolition of duties and made way for the creation of a common market, which came into operation in 1824. Ireland was also to contribute two-seventeenths of the total of national expenditure. The details of this financial programme are complex and subject to continuing debate among economic historians. Two points must be underlined: the economies of Ireland and Great Britain were already strongly bound before Union, but the Act did provide a foundation for the development of the Irish economy along certain lines, and thus ensured that economic debate would be central to critique of the Union.

Moreover, the notion that Ireland could be 'normalized' and pacified through the application of British economic norms was to prove crucial. Nationalists could and did argue that the Irish economy had been damaged by the Act of Union, particularly in the areas of over-taxation and customs and duties. Unionists, even if they conceded that the Irish economy had been harmed by the 1801 legislation, could naturally ask whether a native Irish parliament would have fared any better.

The legislation also united the churches of Ireland and England and guaranteed this to be an 'essential and fundamental part of the Union'. The Act decreed that the churches were to be joined 'for ever', formally incorporating Protestants and Protestantism into the Union settlement. As we shall see, however, this arrangement lasted only 70 years. This subsequent modification demonstrated that the Act itself was alterable, and change could be initiated by a variety of local or cosmopolitan pressures. This in turn encouraged activists on both sides of the debate to consolidate and concentrate their efforts at both Irish and United Kingdom levels. The Irish Question was never restricted to Ireland; as was to become even more apparent in the 19th century, its impact was integral to the politics of the wider United Kingdom.

Chapter 2
The Catholic question

Older discourses of Catholic tendency to rebellion and sedition
found a new currency in the aftermath of 1798 when, despite
evidence to the contrary, blame for the country's near slide into
anarchy was placed by many commentators almost entirely on the
shoulders of Catholics. The events of the late 18th century had
demonstrated that in-built legal and political privilege were not
sufficient in themselves to safeguard Ireland's Protestant minority.
In one sense, the Act of Union was an exercise in straightforward
mathematics. Long fearful of their minority status in Ireland, Irish
Protestants now found themselves in a majority in the Protestant
United Kingdom. This appeared to secure privilege and guaranteed
protection from the Catholic menace.

Catholics, on the other hand, found their status under the Union
both inhibiting and deeply unsettling. Given that Catholic
Emancipation did not follow in the wake of Union, their anxieties
were understandable. The failure to integrate Catholics fully into
new political arrangements was a badly missed opportunity.
Although we cannot be sure that Catholics would have become loyal
and willing servants of the Crown had this been done, there is little
doubt that the accommodation of at least some Catholic grievances
from the outset would have encouraged Catholics to look more
favourably on the new political arrangements. In common with
Protestants, most Irish Catholics had been deeply alarmed by the

events of 1798 and wanted no repeat of that bloody period. The Catholic middle classes knew that their security depended on political and economic stability, and such sentiment was buttressed by a Catholic hierarchy which was deeply opposed to revolutionary activity.

But Catholics were not immune from the radicalization of politics in the last quarter of the 18th century. Influenced by contemporary political language, the increasingly active mercantile and professional classes began to emphasize rights rather than concessions. Expectations had also been raised by the Relief Act, Westminster's apparently softening attitude towards Catholics and talk of emancipation as part of the Union settlement. The frustration of these hopes encouraged a new kind of political activity, and in the first half of the 19th century Ireland witnessed important displays of Catholic power. Catholicism became explicitly linked with political and social reform in ways that were to have profound effects on long-term political strategy and character. Related suggestions of a burgeoning Catholic nationhood disturbed Irish Protestants and contributed to the hardening of political and sectarian divisions.

Catholic Emancipation

The key political issue in the first decades of the 19th century was Catholic Emancipation, not just in Ireland, but from the mid-1820s in British politics too. The term referred to the removal of the final barriers to the admission of Catholics to positions from which they remained excluded by the penal laws. Many of these had been eradicated by the Relief Acts, but important restrictions remained, such as the right to hold senior government offices and to be a judge. Moreover, Catholics were only permitted to sit in the House of Commons if they took the oath of supremacy which was explicitly offensive to the Catholic faith and church.

Penal law enforcement and its impact on Catholics was highly variegated, and modern scholars have emphasized the patchy and unsystematic way in which the laws had been introduced and enforced in the 18th century. But their existence was rooted in deep suspicion of Catholics and a belief in their inherent disloyalty. The Catholics who campaigned for the repeal of these laws were well aware of these attitudes and came increasingly to resent them. The psychological and symbolic impacts of the penal laws were crucial for they reinforced the idea of a beleaguered people. Catholic reformers were able to successfully exploit this.

Daniel O'Connell, known during his career as 'the Councillor' and 'the Liberator', was the undisputed leading light in the campaign for Catholic Emancipation. An extraordinarily charismatic and innovative politician, he was one of the foremost political figures of his generation. Born in County Kerry in 1775, O'Connell belonged to a minor gentry family which had managed to retain its land and increase its fortune despite the penal laws. In common with many members of his family, O'Connell was educated on the Continent, but his brief studies at Douai were interrupted by the excesses of the French Revolution. This was to have an impact on his political strategy: though sympathetic to some of the aims of both the French Revolution and the United Irishmen, he retained a strong aversion to political violence. O'Connell read for the bar in London between 1794 and 1796, and subsequently became one of the best known and most prosperous barristers of his day.

O'Connell's credentials for leadership had been established during the first two decades of the century when he led the opposition to the 'veto', the idea that the government should be able to attach conditions (usually the right to approve clerical appointments and thus ensure a loyal hierarchy) to emancipation legislation. Such vetoes were in fact acceptable in a number of other Catholic countries and hardly unusual for their time. O'Connell's rejection of the veto for Ireland signifies a proto-nationalist element to his emancipation demand. Prominent Irish Catholics in the Catholic Association were divided on this question, but its eventual rejection

2. Daniel O'Connell, known as 'the Liberator' to many of his supporters, was one of Ireland's greatest politicians.

reflected the growing gap between the conservative and the progressive sections of the emancipation movement.

O'Connell began his campaign in earnest in 1823 with the foundation of a new Catholic Association. Through the Association, he successfully linked the question of Catholic Emancipation to the temporal needs and grievances of ordinary Irish Catholics. This was a crucial aspect of his broader strategy as Emancipation would benefit only a tiny section of the Catholic population. By linking it to such issues as rural distress, tithes, and sectarian harassment, he involved people directly in the debate and encouraged the notion that they had a personal stake in its outcome. But he also developed a popular and populist discourse of Catholic disadvantage, of the historical oppression of the Catholic people and their Church. His historical references and collective slogans encouraged the development of a broad, cohesive, and formidable organization. At the same time, however, he retained his loyalty to the Crown and the British constitution, believing it to be flexible and liberal enough to be able to absorb inevitable democratic improvement.

O'Connell's methods were simple and innovative, but they were not without risk. His first great tactic was to introduce the 'Catholic rent'. Before 1824, subscriptions to the Catholic Association had cost one guinea per year; this high fee ensured that its membership would remain small and elite. In 1824 O'Connell reduced the membership charge for the Association to as little as a penny a month. This was a charge that almost everyone could afford and it seemed to be the ideal solution to a number of problems: it helped to refute the claims that the Catholic Association represented only a narrow and unrepresentative section of the Irish population; it raised revenue with which the campaign could be maintained (about £17,000 by March 1825); and it attracted considerable publicity and mass support. Large public meetings were held to demonstrate support for Emancipation and use was made of the press to disseminate political ideas.

Such organization of course anticipated subsequent political mobilization in Ireland, not just because of its broad-based membership, but also because of its integration of the Catholic Church. The Association's fee was collected on Sundays with the help of priests who also aided in publicizing and marshalling the organization. This was not lost on its critics, some of whom viewed the Catholic Association as little more than a direct challenge to the Protestant constitution. Coinciding as it did with an expansion of the Catholic Church and the increasing visibility of a disciplined and more assertive priesthood, Protestant anxieties grew.

By 1825, O'Connell had gained a great deal of publicity and a loyal personal following, but few tangible results for his efforts. After the defeat in the Lords of a Catholic Emancipation Bill that year, it became clear that more had to be done to force concessions. An 1826 election for a Waterford seat provided the forum for a new constitutional experiment. Largely through the initiative of local liberals, Villiers Stuart, a Protestant landlord and supporter of Catholic Emancipation, unseated the anti-Emancipation incumbent. This was a truly significant moment, showing the benefits of a tight and well-organized campaign. It was also an important stage in the increasing Catholicization of the campaign. Despite the fact that Stuart was a Protestant, sectarian slurs were aimed at his opponent and priests helped with lobbying for Stuart. The increasing identification of the campaign with Catholicism, and its corollary, the identification of opponents with Orangeism, gained momentum.

More importantly perhaps, the Waterford success showed that the local Catholic 40-shilling freeholders who had been enfranchised in 1793 could be persuaded to risk the censure of their landlords by voting against their preferred candidate. Such a clear erosion of deference sent shudders not only through Ireland, but through England too. The collection of a new Catholic rent to compensate the Catholic voters who had voted for Stuart and had been victimized as a result did nothing to diffuse the anxieties of critics who saw this as a direct challenge to landed political power. The implications of such unprecedented electoral behaviour were enormous.

The final showdown came in 1828 when O'Connell himself stood for a seat at a County Clare by-election. His opponent, William Vesey Fitzgerald, was an imposing candidate and a supporter of Emancipation, but O'Connell won the election easily. Fitzgerald had the good grace to accept his defeat magnanimously, but facing the electors (and the country) directly rather than making the point through sympathetic Protestant allies represented a major shift and one that presented the government with a real dilemma.

Tension was running high and the question of how Catholics could be appeased while at the same time assuring Protestants that this was no prelude to Catholic domination had to be confronted. Faced by the Waterford victory and fearful of further hostilities (some people were speaking of a revival of civil war), not to mention the election of more and more Catholics and the civil unrest the refusal to admit them to Westminster might cause, the government caved in, bringing forward an Emancipation bill in 1829. A few very senior positions remained closed to Catholics and the Catholic Association was proscribed, but the biggest blow was the disenfranchisement of the 40-shilling freeholders, the constituents who had made the victory possible. This gave some comfort to anxious Protestants.

Although the new legislation would directly affect the lives of very few Catholics, it represented a general victory for Irish Catholicism. Crucial to O'Connell's success had been the tactic – later adopted by Parnell, among others – of backing constitutional politics with an implied threat of violence. Firm organization, the very public and active involvement of the Church in politics, and the very fact that popular pressure had forced a reluctant Westminster to produce the desired bill suggested that the era of democratic Catholic politics had well and truly arrived.

It has often been argued that the manner of the victory was more significant than the fact of it, and there is a great deal of truth in this. The victorious Emancipation crusade gave Irish Catholics a sense that change was possible, that mass association was a powerful weapon, and that the prejudices of the socially and politically privileged could be toppled. It was also a political movement of world significance which demonstrated that democratic and non-revolutionary political organization could move mountains.

Protestant responses

Where did these Catholic successes leave Irish Protestants? They could hardly have failed to have been alarmed at the turn of events, and though O'Connell's public utterances were generally pacific, he could not control the plainly sectarian and triumphalist slogans which were expressed at his meetings. Protestant objections to O'Connell's aims were various. There were of course some opponents who were driven by a basic theological objection to any manifestation of Catholic advancement, but such crude objections to Catholic Emancipation actually enhanced O'Connell's liberal and progressive reputation. More important for Irish Protestants was the effect enhanced political opportunities for Catholics might have on the *status quo*. In addition, the ability of a popular campaign to force through reform which had been resisted by most MPs and Irish Protestants since it had been raised at Westminster suggested that Irish politics might henceforth be decided by agitation rather than legislation.

Protestant culture and organization was profoundly shaped and shaken by O'Connellism, but it also owed its development to a number of other contemporary motivations. Three often related aspects are important: the progress of the Orange Order, the consolidation of Irish Toryism, and the cautious but gradual growth of pan-Protestantism. The Orange Order's relationship to broader Protestant society was ambiguous, and its relationship with both respectable society and Irish Conservatism remained uncertain. Its naked sectarian, violent, and humble beginnings rendered it embarrassing and even objectionable to many Protestants. It was dissolved in 1825 (along with the Catholic Association) and again in 1836, emphasizing its unsavoury reputation and the irritation it caused to the government. But its sustained opposition to Emancipation and later to Repeal helped to erode misgivings, as did the need to present a truly popular movement in the face of a large Catholic majority.

Irish Toryism was the dominant political creed down to 1859, at least in terms of Westminster seats. A popular Toryism was carefully cultivated through such organizations as the Brunswick Clubs, the Irish Protestant Conservative Society, and the Central Conservative Society. Irish Toryism was also influenced by O'Connell's politics and learned much from him about organization and political style: O'Connell's links with the Whigs in the 1830s, for example, encouraged the development of stronger connections between Irish and English Tories. This was to prove crucial in the longer term.

Another important adjustment in this period was increased cooperation between Presbyterians and Anglicans. This was always conditional and cautious, but under the influence of such men as, most famously, Reverend Henry Cooke, some Presbyterians began to abandon their old suspicions of the established Church in the interest of creating a larger and more coherent opposition to Catholic gains. Legislation that appeared to compromise the privileges of the established Church was thus increasingly seen as a generalized attack on Irish Protestantism.

Presbyterian Whig sympathies remained very strong, as did older antagonisms, but both theological shifts within the churches themselves and the threat posed by Catholic triumphalism were powerful incentives to the strengthening of a sense of Protestant resolve, unity, and mission. Irish Protestants had made clear that their resistance to any dismemberment of the Union would not melt away in the face of O'Connell's great show of Catholic strength. This resolve was to shape modern Ireland just as profoundly as that of Irish nationalists.

Repeal

If Catholic Emancipation had not disturbed Protestants enough, the attempt to repeal the Act of Union provided a further and potentially more destructive challenge. After several years of participation in reformist initiatives, some of which threatened Protestant hegemony in local government, O'Connell resurrected the question of repeal (his 1834 repeal motion was defeated decisively in the Commons). Repeal was by no means a clear-cut ambition, not least because what it actually meant seemed to vary according to circumstance and audience. Neither did it follow a logical trajectory, building on 'gains' made in the 1830s. In the broadest sense, it meant the establishment of a Dublin parliament, but a return to the pre-Emancipation parliament was of course unthinkable. O'Connell was himself no separatist and envisaged a political system whereby two legislatures would exist under one Crown. This was to become the basic demand of the most important strand of Irish nationalism for the next 80 years.

In 1840, O'Connell set up the Loyal National Repeal Association and returned to some of the tried and tested methods of agitation he had used to such great effect in the 1820s: huge meetings, clerical involvement and endorsement, and popular and cheap membership for the poor. Despite O'Connell's seeming confidence, it is difficult to see how repeal could have been conceded in the 1840s. The demand represented the dismantling of the Union, and opposition to such a notion, in Ireland and in Britain, was simply insurmountable. In addition, repeal was not simply a matter of civil rights: it could not be presented – as Catholic Emancipation had been – as a logical and just development in the context of a modernizing United Kingdom. Its implications cut to the quick of the British constitution.

As in the 1820s, O'Connell's huge meetings raised the possibility of confrontation, while displaying orderliness and discipline. He was himself careful to stress his opposition to violence and was especially critical of agrarian secret societies which continued to make their presence felt throughout the period. It is in this context that we can understand why in 1843, dubbed 'repeal year' by O'Connell, he cancelled his planned 'Monster meeting' at Clontarf in accordance with Peel's demand. This was to be portrayed by some subsequent advanced nationalists as a significant and almost shameful climb-down, though it is difficult to see what defying the order might have gained. In the short term it encouraged two important developments: the widening of the already evident tensions within the Repeal movement, and Peel's attempts to develop policies which would help to reconcile Catholics to the Union.

Educational disputes

One of Peel's most ambitious and controversial attempts to placate Catholics was through the establishment of the Queen's Colleges in 1845. Education was one of the great political and social questions of the 19th and early 20th centuries. It remained the key question as far as the Catholic hierarchy was concerned. As in Britain, the issue turned on questions of confessional influence. The likely shape and character of the education debate were evident from 1831 when the far-reaching and ambitious National Education System was introduced to Ireland. The main sticking point became – inevitably – a religious one. The primary system was established as strictly non-denominational but, by the second half of the 19th century, it was thoroughly denominationalized. A denunciation of 'mixed-education' (Catholics together with Protestants and later extended to mean women with men, Catholic or Protestant) became a central plank in the Catholic Church's wider agenda, and no politician who hoped to establish friendly relations with the Church could afford to ignore this.

Peel's 1845 legislation envisaged three new, non-denominational colleges, in Belfast, Cork, and Galway. But the religious and political complexion of this scheme brought tensions within the Repeal movement to a head. The debate about the Queen's Colleges also exposed interesting tensions within the Catholic hierarchy, but after some debate the hierarchy (and the Vatican) deemed the Colleges dangerous to the morals of the young and forbade Catholic involvement. Finding support for the scheme to extend Irish higher educational facilities to Catholics was not difficult, but establishing agreement on the structure and administration of any potential college proved impossible. Reconciling Catholics to the Union was evidently going to be a Herculean task.

Young Ireland

One important dissenting faction within the Repeal movement was the Young Ireland group. It is significant that, apart perhaps from the involvement of some Young Irelanders in a 'rising' in 1848, they are probably best known for their literary output, their newspapers, and the links they represented between the past and the future of Irish nationalism. Essentially cultural nationalists, in common with O'Connell, the Young Irelanders appealed to history, but their understanding and use of Ireland's past was but one of the many differences between their aspirations and his. Though an offshoot of the broader Repeal movement, they were more influenced by European and Carlylean Romanticism, and more culturally minded and exclusive, than the main body of the movement.

Thomas Davis, a Protestant, set the tone of the Young Irelanders, espousing a sense of Irish nationhood which depended on cultural distinction – especially through language – as well as some form of political autonomy. He promoted these views through the *Nation*, his influential newspaper which enjoyed a wide audience. A streak of Anglophobia underlined his views, and this was later augmented by John Mitchel, whose own writings were ferociously anti-English and deeply influential for subsequent generations of separatist nationalists.

The Young Irelanders espoused a form of inclusive nationalism which could transcend religious difference, but they had also to face the reality of the increasing Catholicization of national aspirations. An even more awkward detail was that many of the Catholics who were involved in Repeal agitation did not share their lofty ideals. Catholics were largely concerned with the question of winning rights for the majority and not with abstract notions of all-encompassing nationality. Concern for their country and their Church corresponded and could not easily be separated.

Davis found O'Connell's rhetoric to be divisive, even sectarian. This was perhaps an unduly harsh assessment, for O'Connell was no Catholic extremist. But he did articulate his notions of Irish nationhood very much in Catholic terms, claiming in 1826 that, 'the people' were Catholic, and 'the Catholic people of Ireland are a nation'. At the same time, O'Connell was careful to extol the virtues of the liberal Protestants who supported Catholic Emancipation and the nationalist Protestants who supported Repeal. But his approach was far more utilitarian than that of the Young Irelanders. How could 'the nation' be anything but overwhelmingly Catholic given the demographic realities? Was this not a simple case of democratic inevitability?

Such a functional approach did not suit the impatient Young Irelanders, neither did it really clarify O'Connell's own unclear and changeable thinking on the matter. The Queen's Colleges controversy brought many of these latent tensions to the surface. Davis had famously declared 'educate that you might be free', and for him the Colleges offered an outstanding opportunity for Irishmen, Protestant and Catholic, to be educated together, to cultivate inclusiveness, and to build up links of common nationality. O'Connell's siding with the anti-Queen's faction of the hierarchy spelled the end of a connection which was in any case already on the rocks.

The final break came over the use of violence, which O'Connell of course opposed and John Mitchel had begun to openly advocate (as a final resort, he claimed). A rival organization, the Irish Confederation, was formed by some of the disgruntled Young Irelanders in 1847. It was radicalized by the rapidly worsening agrarian crisis, the use of militant rhetoric by some members, and international events. John Mitchel and Thomas Meagher began to promote Irish separatism and, despite internal splits within the Association and the arrest of many of its most prominent activists, a number of members came together for a brief attempt at rebellion in County Tipperary in 1848.

Easily put down, this was little more than a skirmish. But its symbolic value was amplified along with the reputation of many of the Young Irelanders themselves. Their final 'stand' was somewhat farcical, but they exercised considerable influence over subsequent generations of nationalists, partly because Young Ireland and the Confederation encompassed such a large mixture of ideas and opinions: separatism, agrarian radicalism, cultural nationalism, and pluralism. All found their imitators and followers in the ensuing decades.

Chapter 3
Land questions

Ireland's population grew from about 5 million in 1800 to a peak of about 8.2 million in 1841. The convulsions of the famine years encouraged an abrupt drop, but the Irish population continued to decline in every subsequent decade. By 1911, the population stood at about 4.3 million, a little over half of the 1841 figure. This represented a unique demographic pattern in 19th-century Europe, which experienced almost universal population growth.

Ireland's rising population was one of the most important factors shaping social and economic conditions in the mid-19th century. The expansion of the population in an overwhelmingly agricultural country had profound effects on rural life, not least in the area of land division. As the Irish population multiplied, so too did pressure on land. Not everyone believed that Ireland's growing population amounted to over-population, and there is some evidence to suggest that long-term population growth may have stabilized. But optimistic notions of the country's ability to provide enough land and industrial employment to accommodate its population sat uneasily with the reality of the growing subdivision of land holdings, greater dependence on the potato, and the increase in poverty among the poorest sections of the rural population.

Only about one-fifth of Ireland's population lived in towns of 20 or more houses in 1841, and just under 85% lived on the land in 1851. Between 1845 and the eve of the First World War, the proportion of people living in towns of 1,500 or more rose from about one-sixth to one-third. However, with the notable exception of Belfast, Irish cities and towns expanded slowly in comparison with other urban centres around the British Isles. Most became centres of administration, commerce, and education rather than industry, reflecting both the country's relatively poor industrial development outside the northeast and the pivotal roles towns continued to play in the servicing of farmers and the broader agricultural sector.

The failure of the industrial sector to develop as it had in other parts of the United Kingdom has been attributed to a number of factors, including the dearth of such natural resources as coal and iron ore, the lack of an entrepreneurial culture in the largely Catholic south of the country, and poor planning and investment. This question continues to arouse debate among economic historians and, in common with the financial effects of the Act of Union, it has been shaped by political as well as economic considerations. Some Irish industries, including shipbuilding, linen, and brewing, did fare well over the 19th century, and there were periodic booms in industrial activity and profitability in other sectors. But Irish factories and workshops could not provide sufficient employment to stem the tide of emigration; nor could they absorb the pool of surplus agricultural labour that grew rapidly in the first half of the 19th century.

Assessing the level of Irish poverty is a difficult task because of the ambiguity of statistics and the impressionistic nature of anecdotal evidence. The effects, and indeed the existence, of factors such as excessive population expansion, over-dependence on the potato (which could form a crucial part of a generally nutritious diet), the alleged propensity of the Irish to marry young and to rear large families, and the emphasis on tillage rather than pasture have all been subjected to re-evaluation by historians and economists, who continue to disagree on their overall impact.

We can, however, make some general points about the factors that helped to shape the rural economy and the lives of the people who depended upon it. The first is that the Irish economy was already deeply locked into United Kingdom and indeed broader European economic networks which ensured that Irish farmers and manufacturers were subjected to both internal *and* external economic fluctuations. Though Irish farming was probably less backward than is often supposed and some sectors had responded well to the demands of international trade, this could not insulate it from economic crisis. A striking example of this was the sharp economic decline that followed the end of the French Wars from 1815. The second point is that while food shortages and distress were recurrent problems, the lack of resources with which to buy and distribute food had a still more devastating impact. Seasonal unemployment and the remoteness of the poorest areas (especially in the west of the country) exacerbated this. The third is that though industry enjoyed some success, particularly in and around Belfast, Ireland's industrial sector was simply too small to absorb surplus labour at the best of times, let alone in times of acute economic difficulty. The fourth and final point is that while severe economic downturn could affect many thousands of people, the already impoverished suffered most; the plight of the most underprivileged and itinerant was one of the most pressing social problems in pre-Famine Ireland.

The Great Famine, 1845–9

The Great Famine of 1845–9 was modern Ireland's worst catastrophe and indeed the most severe natural disaster in 19th-century Europe. Known also as 'the Great Hunger', the calamity was set off by *Phytophthora infestans*, a fungus which had travelled to Ireland from the Americas, continental Europe, and Great Britain. It attacked potato crops, often with horrific speed, spoiling a crucial source of food for Ireland's population. Over half of 1845's crop was free from the disease, but the following year's almost completely failed. There appeared to be some improvement in 1847, but the acreage planted was very small and shortage was endemic, not least because many hungry people had eaten the seed potatoes which were normally planted. It was not until 1849 that a near-normal crop was reported. The tragedy was compounded by the spread of diseases that affected both rural and urban Ireland.

The Famine cast a long shadow over modern Ireland, its effects reaching deep into the social, political, and economic life of the country, and probably still further into the psyche of its survivors. Though there is still some disagreement about precise figures, any inventory of the demographic impact of the Famine provides a grim reminder of the scale of tragedy that unfolded in Ireland in the 1840s: about one million dead through starvation and disease; the emigration of around 1.5 million in the ten years between 1845 and 1855; and the decline of cottiers or labourers, already disadvantaged as the poorest section of the agrarian hierarchy. The horrendous deaths of some of the people who were crammed aboard the 'coffin ships' bound for America also left a lasting legacy of bitterness.

A controversial debate has grown up around the question of the adequacy and effectiveness of the relief measures introduced by British governments during the crisis. No 19th-century British government was prepared to throw limitless amounts of money at 'Irish problems', but the Famine governments could not be accused of outright callous negligence. Prime Ministers Peel and Lord John Russell from 1846 initiated schemes including public works programmes and the massive distribution of free food from 1847, but these could never in themselves hope to quell the tide of death and wretchedness, and they were never intended to provide cures for Ireland's many ills. They were inhibited by structural difficulties, inefficient organization, and a serious shortage of food in Europe. The scale and extent of relief schemes were also constrained by a profound reluctance to upset the economic *status quo* which, it was believed, could send both the British and Irish economies into freefall. The overall effectiveness of relief efforts was also hampered by delays, bureaucratic incompetence and insensitivity, and the

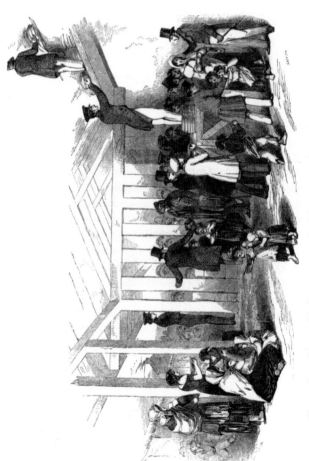

3. A 1847 illustration of a soup kitchen, set up to feed the starving in Cork.

mistaken decision to suspend all aid before the crisis had receded. Sadly, relief was for many degrading, inadequate, and slow to arrive.

Much compassionate and generous work was done by individuals and charities, most notably the Quakers, and there is little doubt that unlike some of their Whitehall counterparts, Irish administrators battled heroically to feed as many of the starving as possible. But the Famine years were also marked by greed and self-interest. Some individuals ruthlessly gained from soaring food prices and the availability of an impoverished and desperate workforce, while others profited from misery by providing loans and food at highly inflated rates. Eviction rates increased, the religious or political creed of farmers and landlords bearing little relation to their propensity to evict tenants, who faced an uncertain future to say the least. In this context, emigration was not only a sensible option, but a blessing for the many people who were desperate to escape from their austere and uncertain existence.

Emigration

In common with numerous of their European neighbours, millions of Irish people sought opportunities and better conditions abroad. Emigration became a well-established fact of Irish life, touching the lives of most men and women no matter what their confessional, political, or economic circumstances. Psychological as well as geographic frontiers were traversed and negotiated as generations of Irish people were reared in the expectation that they too would join the exodus. At least 8 million men and women left Ireland between 1801 and 1921, and Irish people were easily the most likely of all Europeans to leave the continent in the second half of the 19th century.

Numbers of Irish men and women – particularly northern Presbyterians – had sailed for North America in the 18th century, but Great Britain attracted the overwhelming majority of emigrants.

4. This depiction of a family being evicted due to non-payment of rent during the Famine was one of many such images produced during and after the crisis.

Some of this movement was seasonal, but there also developed permanent 'Irish communities' in British cities, notably in London, Manchester, and Liverpool. The flow of emigrants from Ireland to Britain and the New World expanded rapidly in the first half of the 19th century – some 1.5 million left Ireland between 1815 and the Great Famine – assisted partly by cheaper and safer passage and a growing understanding of prospects abroad.

The numbers of people leaving depended heavily upon fluctuating economic and social conditions, both in Ireland and in potential host countries. Destination was influenced by the cost of travel, the availability of work, the willingness of host countries to take them, and, most importantly, by the networks and patterns established by earlier émigrés. Canada, Australia, and South America provided new homes for many thousands of Irish expatriates at different times, but the United States was to become by far the most common destination for Irish people travelling beyond Europe after about 1870.

Comparisons with emigration from other European countries during the same period reveal a number of peculiarly Irish features: family or group migration was relatively low, the number of unattached women was higher than usual (young unmarried adults formed the bulk of emigrants, and women were as likely as men to leave over most of the period), and Irish expatriates were less likely to return home than most other Europeans; those who did go back usually did so as visitors rather than permanent re-settlers. The men and women who left Ireland also tended to be unskilled, often describing themselves as labourers or servants (though some textile skills were exported). This may have been related to the fact that though every Irish county was affected by high levels of emigration from the 1840s, most – though not all – émigrés were drawn from the least privileged counties, being most prone to the twin incentive of rural poverty and a dearth of alternative employment.

The question of why people left is far more complex, and certainly much less obviously political, than is sometimes assumed. Irish people did not primarily leave their homes because they were pushed or deliberately starved out. The vast majority left because Ireland could not guarantee them all or some of: land, work, marriage partners, the opportunity for advancement, and a decent standard of living. Moreover, as emigration became more and more established as a normal aspect of Irish life, the link between the state of the Irish economy and the decision to leave the country diminished. In addition, increasing proficiency in English and improved literacy rates across the 19th century ensured that Irish emigrants were better prepared for the New World than many of their more linguistically, ethnically, and religiously diverse European neighbours.

Many nationalists disapproved of migration, arguing that it was the wicked and inevitable product of British misgovernment. But their censure did not stop people from leaving in enormous numbers. That some landlords advocated assisted emigration at times has tended to overshadow the fact that so too did some nationalists and many priests. Assistance for emigrants came, at different times, from the state, landlords, charities, host countries, and clerics; by far the most funds were provided by those who had already left to those who lacked the funds rather than the will to follow.

The social and economic impact on Ireland of emigration is still more difficult to quantify. It would be erroneous to assert that Ireland's émigrés possessed skills or assets whose removal weakened the country's economic development; the emigration of the poor and unskilled was only exacerbated by the Famine. It does, however, seem that some more comfortable farmers did in fact take their families abroad as a result of the profound uncertainty produced by the Famine. Though that crisis abated, a partial return to normality was no guarantee against future catastrophe and could hardly compete with the strong appeal of 'a better life' elsewhere. This attraction remained seemingly irresistible until very late in our period.

Post-Famine conditions

The fact that a broad swathe of conditions appeared to improve in the aftermath of the Famine was both a product of that catastrophe and an extension of earlier trends. The already evident tendency for people to marry late or not at all intensified, and the move from tillage to pasture was reinforced. One in four farms disappeared between 1845 and 1851, dependence on the potato declined, and there was a marked drop in the number of farms under 15 acres. The death or emigration of so many of the poorest citizens decreased the pressure on land and removed a significant proportion of surplus labour. As a result, real living standards and wages probably increased and the task of consolidating and modernizing Irish agriculture seemed more feasible. However, post-Famine improvement must not be exaggerated. Although emigration had clearly benefited large numbers of people, it was in itself no answer to persistent Irish rural problems and the overall question of Irish poverty. The departure of large numbers of people from the most impoverished districts did not eradicate rural joblessness, and it could be argued that large-scale emigration actually militated against the modernization of the rural economy.

The huge reduction in the numbers of the labouring and cottier class was one of the most important social and economic products of the Great Famine. The intensification of the consolidation of farms was another prominent development, as was the appearance of large cattle ranches. The reduction of subdivision and over-reliance on crops for cash was possible because of population decline, but it was also encouraged by international prices and market demand for such Irish goods as meat, milk, and butter. But consolidation was no more a panacea than emigration, especially as it appeared to be an exceptional post-Famine phenomenon. The decline of many traditional rural customs, the shrinking number of Irish language speakers, and, conversely, rising literacy rates all owed much to the experience of the Famine years; tragically, each was paid for most dearly by the disappearance of the poorest, who were most likely to be illiterate, Irish speaking, and landless.

Yet, post-Famine Ireland was a changed place in ways which defy quantification. The catastrophe of the 1840s cast ever more attention on the state of Ireland's economy and land tenure system. What we now know as the 'Land Question' was ultimately solved by state-sponsored peasant proprietorship, but earlier initiatives had focused on reforming the tenurial relationship in a way that did not upset the fundamental sanctity of property rights. Until the 1870s, parliamentary involvement reflected a concern with landlords' roles rather than tenant farmers'. However, more radical ideas were increasingly being initiated and debated from within Ireland.

One of the earliest manifestations of this was the Irish Tenant League, established in 1850. The Tenant League was notable because it attempted to transform an issue with much local support to a national platform. It demanded the legalization of 'tenant right' or 'Ulster Custom', which allowed an outgoing tenant to sell the occupancy of his holding to the highest bidder, and in some cases thus to secure compensation from landlords for improvements. Though mainly found in Ulster, this was in fact practised in other parts of Ireland. It was believed by many to have contributed to the more peaceful and economically stable state of the northern counties and to the general prosperity of the province. Recent research has disputed this; nevertheless, it became a popular catch-cry of many land activists, serving as a useful slogan which encompassed a number of demands.

More importantly, it underscored the idea that British economic ideology was unsuitable for Irish circumstances and that the rights of property as recognized in British law should be liable to modification which would take account of the customary and everyday practices of Irish tenants. Such demands sought in reality to enhance the farmer's stake in the soil by diluting the legal authority of its owners; a radical aim indeed. The Tenant League strove to win support from tenant farmers from the north and the south of the country, but any unity which it generated was transitory. It did, however, provide stimulus for the growing role of the strong farmer in Irish politics and the need to establish an independent political grouping which would represent Irish grievances in the imperial parliament.

Landlords and tenants

If land was to be made into a political issue, guilty men had to be identified and indicted. Almost uniquely, large numbers of nationalist polemicists, individual tenant farmers, and successive British governments were able to agree that Irish landlords should be held accountable for Ireland's undeveloped rural sector. The way that historians customarily assessed the role and economic performance of Irish landlords, once vilified as ruthless, feckless absentees, was transformed in the late 20th century. Modern historians have tended to emphasize the very considerable difficulties faced by landlords, whose place in Irish society was complicated and undermined by their religion (most were Anglican), their background, and their seeming detachment from the day-to-day reality of their fellow countrymen and -women. There is now a greater appreciation of diversity of status, outlook, and circumstance among landlords. Contemporary English commentators, on the other hand, more straightforwardly wondered why Irish landlords were not more like their English counterparts, who seemed, on the whole, to have adapted well to the challenges of modern agriculture and industry. They condemned the seeming unwillingness of Irish landowners to take a more active – indeed paternalistic – role in ensuring the wellbeing of their tenants. Irish landlords, it seemed, were exercising the rights of property without exercising its duties as they were understood in England.

There was, however, no general consensus about what a 'good' landlord actually was, none at least which corresponded with the requirements and wishes of both landowners and tenants. For their part, landlords resented the tendency of British governments and rational commentators to fail to recognize the difficulties they encountered. There was a crucial dearth of investment and modernization of property, but this was difficult for all but large landowners, given the relatively low level of rental return on Irish property. Innovation, improvement, and attempts to curb subdivision were often thwarted by tenants suspicious of new practices, and absenteeism in itself did not guarantee poor land management (in fact, absentees were quite popular in some areas where tenants relished their relative freedom from landlord interference). In addition, Irish land could not hope to employ the whole of the growing population, and industry could not absorb the excess.

Rents in fact rose less than agricultural prices down to 1880. Large-scale eviction was not endemic, though it did increase sharply during the Great Famine. It usually took place only when tenants repeatedly refused or were unable to pay their rent. Nonetheless, landlords should not be let entirely off the hook. As a class, they were undoubtedly inadequate and underinvesting managers; some of their extravagance was legendary and incompatible with sound land management and agricultural stability. Moreover, as a class they were noticeably rich. Though their status was increasingly challenged and whittled down by the rising Catholic middle classes, landlords continued to wield significant social influence and played a disproportionately important role in parliamentary politics until 1874 (the number of landlords who were MPs fell from 73 in 1868 to 52 in 1874). Perhaps even more importantly, though their actual social, political, and economic power diminished over the century, they were still perceived to be excessively influential and privileged, thus providing ammunition for the envious and ambitious.

The Famine marked the end of an era for some of Ireland's less financially secure landowning families and a tentative change in the approach of British government. In keeping with their views about the responsibilities of landowners, much of the burden of the poor law system was placed firmly on the shoulders of property. This system – largely unsuitable for Ireland since its introduction in 1838 and a classic example of the propensity of British governments to introduce patently unsuitable legislation to Ireland (even in the face of expert advice) – was severely stretched during the Famine years as many ratepayers, especially in the poorest districts, simply could not pay. By 1843, large numbers of landlords were already indebted; high rates bills and the loss of rents during the Famine propelled more of them into arrears. A striking admission of the failure of Irish property was demonstrated by the Encumbered Estates Act of 1849 which allowed the landed classes to sell their debt-burdened land more easily than hitherto. By 1857, over 3,000 sales had been made under the Act, but it failed to be the antidote to an endemic problem. Neither did it attract a new and more enterprising landlord class to Ireland.

Devising a solution to Ireland's chaotic tenurial system was one of the major tasks faced by successive governments under the Union. The key consideration for all British administrations was the pacification and improvement of Irish society so as to make it both more easily governable and more amenable to British rule. However, the slow pace of reform, a perception of the inviolability of property, and the deep reluctance to propose the drastic solutions which were needed encouraged the increasing radicalization of a question which continued to gain political currency.

Parliamentary interference offered no easy solution as no legislation could hope to encompass, let alone govern, the intensely complicated nature of day-to-day landlord–tenant relations, which varied enormously over the country. Landowners' absolute legal authority was as subject to informal modification, compromise, and outright antagonism as the wider Irish economy was to international forces. Rural violence and off-the-record compromise represented an unofficial acceptance of this uneasy situation, but the legislative and intellectual tide began to turn more obviously from the mid-1860s, when the focus shifted from the rights and duties of property to the appeasement of an increasingly politicized tenantry.

Solving the land question

Any attempt to interfere with property rights was bound to produce some disaffection in English political circles as well as in some Irish ones, but this was broadly the course taken by a succession of British administrations, albeit in an initially cautious form. The settlement of the land question was a central plank in Gladstone's mission to 'pacify Ireland', but his bills were watered down in 1870 by cabinet opposition and in 1881 by Lords' amendments. His 1870 Land Act stopped short of legalizing tenant right, but agreed that it should be recognized where it already existed, and, most importantly, the Act introduced some measures for tenant land purchase. This Act was an overwhelming disappointment whose terms were prohibitive. Neither did it address the question of rent control, which many landlords believed to be the same as rent reduction. It did, however, augur a new era of land legislation which would fundamentally alter Ireland's landholding system.

Gladstone famously declared himself 'quite contented with the social condition of Ireland and the prospects of its future solid happiness' during his one and only visit to Ireland in 1877. It was in fact in 1877 that the fragile bubble of relative prosperity began to burst. By 1879, Ireland was in the midst of a severe agricultural depression and a Land War. The Land League won a major concession through Gladstone's 1881 Land Act (the political circumstances which influenced the Land War will be considered in more detail in the next chapter). This instituted a system of dual ownership and the regulation of rents by special tribunals. The main beneficiaries of this legislation were larger farmers, the very constituency most likely to become the most valuable and loyal Home Rulers. The embourgeoisment of Irish nationalism meant that rural prosperity became more closely linked with constitutional politics, thus creating networks of mutually beneficial ties and loyalties.

Though the actual economic and social consequences of the 1881 Act are debatable, at the very least it must be seen as a crucial step in the gradual erosion of landlordism in Ireland. This was by no means an even process and there was no sudden transfer of land from landlords to tenants, but it was an ongoing development which culminated in the great Land Purchase Act of 1903. This definitively established land purchase as the final solution to the land question, reasserting the primacy of property rights by creating a new class of owner. The key to making the system of land transfer work was to induce tenants to buy and landlords to sell. It seems that both were willing to do so, but only if the price were right and it took massive intervention from the British Treasury to accomplish this. Almost 300,000 sales were completed under the 1903 Act, most between 1906 and 1908, and by the eve of the First

World War, three-quarters of tenants were in the process of buying out landlords.

The 1903 Act, and the acts which subsequently refined it, represented the culmination of a truly remarkable shift in thinking about Ireland's tenurial arrangements, not only among British politicians, but also among Irish farmers, nationalists, and landlords themselves. The notion that improving landlordism might solve the problem had been replaced by the far more radical conviction that only dismantling landlordism would do. The Land League played a major role in this shift by increasing expectations about further reform and by establishing peasant proprietorship as a real aim. The convergence of the land and national questions was in fact well in place from the 1860s, but this relationship was cemented by a Land League that showed that the putting aside (however temporarily) of local rivalries in the interest of a common cause could actually force real legislative concessions. This helped to close the gap between rural Ireland and its largely urban parliamentary representatives, in the process creating something of a nationalist, if not a national, community.

Chapter 4
National questions

As long as Irish men and women remained unconvinced of the
benefits of Union, calls for its removal or reform would continue.
Vigorous political debate of the kind seen in the 1820s to the early
1840s had withered away in the face of the devastation of the Great
Famine. But the fact that O'Connell's Repeal movement faltered
during the crisis reflected the alarm and shifting priorities of many
of his supporters, especially the poorer and more vulnerable ones,
rather more than it signalled the disappearance of political
consciousness. Importantly, too, the Famine had itself come to
reinforce the idea that arguments for the advantages of Union
were intellectually and politically indefensible.

This encouraged a new period of intense debate about the
constitutional relationship between Ireland and Great Britain.
The political reins were taken up by a variety of players with
sometimes incompatible aims and methodologies, but, despite
some differences, what emerged was the increasing Catholicization
of the national question. Confessional considerations would
continue to colour every component of the wider nationalist
campaign, from land reform to education, from cultural
nationalism to constitutional politics and republicanism. Some
attempts were made to counter this process, but very few leading
political figures could escape the practical necessity of keeping
political aspirations and tactics within margins acceptable to the

Catholic Church. The Church's harshest disapproval was, however, to be reserved for plainly revolutionary societies, while it drew, eventually, ever closer to constitutional nationalism.

Physical force nationalism

One of the greatest political threats identified by the Irish Catholic hierarchy was the Fenian movement, a political creed whose core objectives appeared to enjoy little success, but whose constituency – if not its aims and methods – in fact reflected much of the outlook of the wider Irish population. Fenianism was born of the devastation of the Famine and the failure of the Young Ireland Rising, and of a volatile international situation in which troubled British relations with America and France promised opportunities to Irish conspirators. The military and strategic bungling that characterized the 1848 Rising served to promote a tight and secretive culture within a movement which was decidedly wary of infiltration and incompetence. Yet, it was military failure *par excellence* which was to teach Fenianism its most important lessons and to guide it down new political paths.

Fenianism was the general term for organizations founded in Ireland and America in 1858/59 which were variously known as the Irish Republican Brotherhood (IRB), the Irish Revolutionary Brotherhood, or simply and perhaps more ominously as 'the Organization'. It was a secret, revolutionary grouping (organized in 'cells' and 'circles') under whose roof sheltered a number of influences and objectives which were bound by their Anglophobia, their disgust at self-seeking and ineffective Irish MPs, and their militant commitment to an Irish Republic. Through former members of the Irish Confederation, most notably James Stephens, lessons about European conspiratorial movements were learned and international links were forged. The most important of these was the American connection, which was to provide men, money, and political direction. Others, including John O'Donovan Rossa and Charles Kickham, were literary men as well as insurrectionists.

Gaelic culture and history inspired some; John O'Mahoney, for example, came up with the Fenian label, basing it on the 'Fianna', a mythical Celtic military force. The many memoirs, manifestos, novels, and plays produced by Fenians, coupled with Stephens' newspaper *Irish People*, ensured that Fenianism left a potent literary and polemical legacy.

The social context of Fenianism can be traced to the changing social and economic conditions of post-Famine Ireland. Emigration, often seen as an opportunity rather than a punishment, was portrayed by Fenians and their sympathizers as a by-product of British malevolence. Though most Irish-Americans probably did not immerse themselves in Irish organizations or political societies, home-sickness and disorientation could be converted into political energy; having prospered abroad or having failed to do so could equally translate into a desire to highlight the iniquity of the British presence in Ireland. Irish adherents were overwhelmingly drawn from the country's expanding and increasingly self-confident petit bourgeoisie; the artisans, publicans, clerks, and shopkeepers of market towns were strongly represented in a movement which boasted around 54,000 members by the mid-1860s. Rising real wages, improving living standards, and the gradual breakdown of traditional patterns of deference fuelled the growth of Fenianism. So too did a desire for rational entertainment, for political education and debate, and for status within one's community and among one's peers.

It is difficult to disagree with William O'Brien's assessment that 'it was not the deeds of Fenianism which counted, but the spirit'. The vast majority of Fenians did not become involved in the organization's more spectacular political activities, which appeared to receive little support from the Irish population and brought about widespread condemnation in Britain. Most famous among these was the long-awaited Fenian Rising of 1867, strongest in Dublin but also staged in other parts of the country. Fewer than 10,000 men probably turned out to rebel against the British presence in Ireland. The Rising was only one of a number of extravagant episodes orchestrated and manipulated by the Fenians. Other important incidents included impressive funerals, support campaigns for Fenian prisoners, and the crucial elevation to martyr status of three men executed after their involvement in the rescue of Fenian prisoners during which an unarmed police guard had been killed.

The wide public support for and interest in such episodes produced a re-casting of Irish nationalism into a blatant but evidently appealing formula: it was Ireland against England, it was politics at its rawest but also at its most difficult to counteract. Fenian activity was easily slotted into a powerful chronology of Irish resistance: 1798, 1803, 1848, and 1867 could and would be marketed as integral parts of the broader history of 700 years of opposition to British oppression. More difficult to convert into popular opinion was the anti-confessionalism of Fenianism. Though it was as an organization dedicated to Tone's and Young Ireland's non-sectarian principles, it was only the more erudite and better known Fenians who publicly challenged clerical involvement in politics. The fact that the Catholic hierarchy condemned the IRB because of its secretive and revolutionary composition fuelled antagonism, but the key point of difference was the degree and direction of clerical involvement rather than the fact of involvement itself. The hierarchy's direct involvement in organizations like the National Association were stark reminders that the Catholic Church was neither immune from nor uninterested in political activity.

Constitutional nationalism

The dazzling displays of resistance staged by some Fenians should not eclipse the hard and often dull work done by individual activists at local levels and the gradual reshaping of the movements which were to lead to more conventional political activity. Neither should it be emphasized at the expense of other innovative and influential political programmes, some of which were to combine to create the most powerful nationalist organization Ireland had known. The always rocky but ultimately creative affiliation between the physical force nationalism of the Fenians and the moral force nationalism of constitutionalists, which developed over the second half of the 19th century, owed much to the post-1867 adjustments within the IRB itself.

In 1873 the organization's Supreme Council cleared the way for association with lawful political activity and agreed that insurrection could be postponed until (the unlikely event that the) support for such an endeavour won the approval of the Irish people. Fenian military planning had been predicated on the assumption that Britain would at some stage be at war – most likely with France or America – and thus vulnerable. By 1867, this had become highly improbable, and still less likely by 1870. The debacle of 1867 had made plain the pointlessness of taking on the British militarily, especially without large-scale support on the ground: shifting social and economic conditions were subsequently calculated and exploited in the process of exploring new political paths.

A leading light in this renovation of nationalist politics was Isaac Butt, an often neglected figure whose respectful attitude towards the British constitution and often erratic behaviour and rakish personal life contributed to the downgrading of his reputation. A Protestant, a brilliant lawyer, and a conservative, Butt's political transformation had taken him from anti-O'Connellism to a defence of the Young Irelanders after the 1848 Rising. Butt remained a committed unionist, but he also became a leading advocate of Union reform. He believed that Irish prosperity could only be guaranteed if the country retained the imperial connection, and maintained that the Union had failed Ireland because of its misapplication and not because of its inherent erroneousness. His task was therefore two-fold: he had to convince Britain to reform the Union, and he had to convince Ireland that the Union was both capable and worthy of salvation. The logic of this was a form of federalism; an Irish parliament which would manage domestic affairs within the context of and subject to the ultimate authority of the imperial parliament.

Butt's preferred method of convincing sceptics of the righteousness of his cause was parliamentary. In 1870 he presided over the foundation of the Home Government Association, which was replaced in 1873 by the more centralized Home Rule League. He attempted to tap into the anxieties and prejudices of a variety of Irish minds: his biggest challenge was to attract both Catholic and Protestant support, and in this way he was an inheritor of a long tradition of attempts to promote pluralist nationalism. But unlike some of his predecessors, he offered, albeit obliquely, somewhat different incentives to each denomination while crowning each with the ultimate prize – an independent Irish parliament. He had the intelligence to recognize that such a strategy was essential if he was to be able to attract a genuinely broad consensus; a simple appeal to common nationality was going to cut little ice in an increasingly polarized country whose main nationalist organizations offered very little to Irish Protestants. It was hopeless, of course, but Butt's association did seem for a short time at least – quite uniquely – to offer something to both bitter opponents of the Union and to those who hoped to put Anglo-Irish relations on a more equal and mutually beneficial footing.

Butt's most strategically important and long-lasting legacy to Irish nationalism was the alliance he formed with Fenianism. This association was, however, to push the constitutional nationalist movement in a direction which virtually assured its radicalization, Catholicization, and consequent loss of most of the Protestant support it had managed to garner. A fundamental product of Fenianism's post-1867 reorganization was the acknowledgement that it would support all movements which strove for even partial Irish independence so long as they did not compromise the IRB itself. A contingent of Fenians and Fenian sympathizers thus embraced constitutionalism, standing for and taking up seats in the imperial parliament.

This unprecedented constitutional-republican parliamentary experiment failed, not least because Butt was increasingly deemed too radical by his conservative and mainly Protestant supporters, and at the same time too timid by the militant and the impatient within his parliamentary grouping. What emerged was something of a showdown between, on the one hand, Butt's careful, respectable, and gradualist parliamentary activity and, on the other, a radical wing impatient with an approach which offered little evidence that any fundamental constitutional change was forthcoming.

Led by the Fenian, Joseph Biggar, who was soon joined by Charles Stewart Parnell (a Wicklow Protestant landlord), and later by Frank Hugh O'Donnell, a rogue element of Butt's party began to win considerable publicity for its policy of obstruction. Though he had himself earlier toyed with some form of parliamentary obstruction, Butt disapproved deeply of the assault on parliamentary convention perpetrated by the radicals in his party. But his condemnation could not halt the development of a new form of constitutional nationalism. Formulated in opposition to Butt's variety of nationalism, as we shall see, Parnellism was nonetheless built on foundations laid by the moderate Butt and transformed into Ireland's most dynamic political movement since O'Connellism.

The New Departure

Parnell's major political accomplishment was his ability to forge strategically vital alliances, or at least to recognize them as important when they presented themselves to him. His contemporaries and subsequent historians have engaged in endless debates about Parnell's aims, methods, and exact political positioning. The main point of discrepancy seems to turn on whether he was in fact a constitutional nationalist who aimed to secure Home Rule within an imperial context, or whether his ultimate goal was something altogether more ambitious and revolutionary. His flirtation and cooperation with the IRB, his willingness to make inflammatory speeches – to select audiences, it should be noted – and his own refusal to be conclusively pinned down (until about 1886) on the issue have encouraged such debate. This kind of speculation was, of course, engendered by Parnell himself. A cool, aloof, and opportunistic politician, his genius was precisely his ability to avoid fixed labels and thus to retain an independence of action and thought which allowed him to react to specific circumstances as they emerged. This approach helped him to maintain the support of a wide variety of constituencies who could – or convinced themselves that they could – claim him as a fellow traveller.

Parnell's first important alliance was formed in 1879 in the form of a five-point pact with advanced nationalists. His flamboyant disregard for parliamentary procedure (he and his colleagues had kept the House in session for 45 hours in July 1877) and his cordial relations with the Fenian element in the Irish Party won the approval of some leading physical force men, most notably Michael Davitt, chief arms purchaser for the IRB until 1870 and a Fenian felon and exile until his return to Ireland in 1879, and John Devoy, a leading member of Clan na Gael, a secret American republican and revolutionary organization. Known as the 'New Departure', this agreement added a crucial commitment to land agitation to the constitutional–advanced nationalist relationship. This was to be the nexus around which constitutional nationalism would finally establish itself as a potent force that British governments could ill afford to ignore.

The terms of the New Departure included: the end of the federal demand and a declaration in favour of self-government; vigorous agitation of the land question; the exclusion of all sectarian issues; an insistence that Irish members vote together, pursue aggressive tactics, and resist coercion; and advocacy of struggling nationalities in the Empire and elsewhere. This was an explicit rejection of Butt's strategy and an insistence (especially in the rhetoric about sectarianism) on the continuation of the IRB principle, but no resolve on aggressive diplomacy could disguise the fact that advanced nationalists had become constitutionalists in all but name. The IRB's own Supreme Council rejected the New Departure, but it agreed that individual Fenians would be permitted to participate in electoral politics. The revolutionary spirit was kept alive in rhetoric and in deed, but plans for an Irish republic born of revolutionary struggle were, for the time being at least, put aside in the interest of practical politics. Parnell's greatest achievement was to preside over a movement which contained such a staggering array of tensions and contesting ambitions.

The Fenians proved valuable and largely willing allies for Parnell. American money and local connections were vital components of the larger Parnellite operation. In exchange, Parnell agreed to adopt the land as a sectional question of the kind and scale which Butt had avoided. In the process, he presided over the transformation of constitutional politics into a national and implicitly Catholic movement. It is important to emphasize that no clear correlation existed between land agitation and nationalism. As we have seen, rural protest and violence had a long pedigree in Ireland and most such activity was manifestly not an expression of a yearning for Irish autonomy; rather it was commonly a reaction to local conditions and specific circumstances. This does not mean that rural Ireland was uniformly uninterested in wider national questions, but it does suggest that the yoking of the two issues required planning, hard work, and a measure of luck. A severe agricultural slump provided the context for this amalgamation; political opportunism and inspired leadership provided the means.

Land War strategy was in itself quite simple: tenants were to refuse to pay unjust rents and to socially ostracize those who did so. But this of course required enormous amounts of organization and significant injections of cash. It also required the fostering of cooperation between social groups which were traditionally suspicious of each other; the ability to create a functioning united front was probably the Land League's greatest success. Parnell's IRB allies proved invaluable in this area, especially as numbers of Fenians based in Ireland's rural districts and small towns had been active in land agitation for some time. This was a less glamorous occupation than plotting rebellion, but far more functional during the period 1879–82.

Many individual and even some communal ambitions – both personal and national – were undoubtedly sacrificed at the altar of this greater collective endeavour, and some activists – particularly

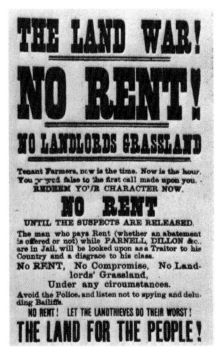

5. A Land League poster of 1881 which coincided with the arrest of Parnell and some of his lieutenants.

Michael Davitt and Anna Parnell (Charles's sister) – hoped that the Land War would in fact lead if not to full-scale revolution, then to a more radical land settlement at the very least. Parnell's swift winding down of the pioneering Ladies' Land League, which had been founded by Anna Parnell, was a telling indication of both his impatience with continuing agitation and his determination to control the wider movement, especially its finances. Members of the Ladies' Land League were dismayed at Parnell's tacit acceptance of Gladstone's 1881 Land Act and of an unofficial deal made between the two men which allowed for Parnell's release from prison and further land reform in exchange for the winding down of rural agitation. Dissidents aside, however, it was clear that Parnell was very much in charge of this operation, and it was he who skilfully shepherded the Land League away from outright insurgency and down a constitutional route whose ultimate destination was Home Rule.

A union of hearts?

Parnell had become leader of the Irish Party in 1880 and election results from that year until just before his death in 1891 confirmed that he was the unchallenged leader of nationalist Ireland. Under his stewardship, the Irish Party's share of the vote increased to 86 seats in 1886, and by-election results confirmed that Catholic Ireland remained loyal to 'the Chief'. In 1884, he strengthened the Party's relationship with the Catholic hierarchy by pledging to support its educational demands in the parliament, thus forming another crucial alliance.

Parnell presided over a political party which was transformed from a loose and undisciplined body into a distinctly tight political machine. This was one of his greatest achievements and probably his most important legacy to the longer history of Irish parliamentary politics. MPs were bound by oath to vote collectively; some financial assistance was made available to those MPs who required it, and the National League – which replaced the Land

6. A map printed in the *Weekly Freeman* featuring the nationalists who were elected in 1886. This map no doubt raised unionist apprehensions.

League in 1882 – became increasingly centralized and controlled (authoritarian, some complained). This maintenance of an ordered and efficient political party was vital, for tight organizational structure was necessary if rogue elements were to be kept in check and if the party was to function as a genuinely independent entity which could bargain with and play off the major British parties.

This strategy seemed to have paid off by 1885–6. After a brief and disappointing flirtation with the Conservative Party, the Irish Party made an alliance with Gladstone's Liberals, forming what became known as a 'union of hearts'. Gladstone embraced Irish Home Rule, but the alliance proved to be anything but painless: it was to split the Liberals and helped to send them into the political wilderness for over 20 years. It also cost the Irish Party the measure of independence it had cultivated. Gladstone's 'conversion' to Irish Home Rule may be best understood as a culmination of his Irish policy, which had begun with the disestablishment of the Church of Ireland in 1869 and which was augmented by his own preference for devolutionary forms of governance. He was impatient with the frequent clogging up of parliamentary time and political energy by Irish questions, and became convinced of the truth of the Irish Party's claim to represent the will of the majority of the Irish people. Gladstone's own enthusiasm could not, however, guarantee the successful passage of his 1886 Home Rule Bill, hindered as it was by strong opposition in both houses. It was defeated in the Commons by 343 votes to 311.

Unionist opposition

The anti-Home Rule majority in the House of Lords would see off any bill that might make it through the Commons – as it did in 1893 – but unionists nonetheless responded to the news of Gladstone's conversion with alarm and a flurry of activity. Liberal Protestants were especially incensed, resulting in the virtual decimation of liberal influence in Ireland, particularly in Ulster. The most obvious manifestations of these anxieties were the

WELCOME TO HAWARDEN

IRISH AFFAIRS

"**GOOD HEALTH!**"

7. Parnell and Gladstone raise their glasses to the 'union of hearts' and to a mutually agreeable settlement of Irish affairs.

National questions

foundation of the Ulster Loyalist Anti-Repeal Committee and the Ulster Unionist Parliamentary Party, both of which built on the work of some of the organizations that had opposed Repeal.

Home Rule was perceived by Protestants to be an expression of Catholic power, notwithstanding the soothing words of Parnell and some of his lieutenants. It is thus unsurprising that the rumours and then confirmation of Gladstone's stance should promote a Protestant alliance which largely transcended theological, social, and economic differences. Protestant churches, grandees, industrialists, and workers could find common cause in the threat of Home Rule (or 'Rome Rule'), though older disagreements would resurface after the crisis had passed. English Conservative allies such as Lord Randolph Churchill encouraged both their collaboration and their resistance, fostering a mutually useful alliance between Conservatives and unionists, an alliance that was to keep a Home Rule bill at bay until 1912.

PARNELLITE INVASION
OF ULSTER.

TO THE ORANGEMEN
AND LOYALISTS OF DOWN AND ULSTER.

BRETHREN AND FRIENDS,

On the 2nd of December last, a threatened **Invasion of our Loyal** Province by the Parnellites, through her Frontier stronghold of the Town of Newry, was prohibited by Her Majesty's Government, and we therefore counselled you to abstain from holding the Loyal counter Demonstration which had been arranged.

The **PARNELLITES** have announced a **Meeting, designated as an** adjournment of their former dis-loyal meeting to be held on the Lord's Day, 1st June next.

The objects of the **Disloyal Meeting on Sunday next are to flaunt the** flag of Sedition and Socialism in our midst and to effect the dismemberment of this Glorious Empire. Shall this be permitted without a protest on our part?

NO, NEVER!

Are the very bonds of society and the preservation of the Public Peace to be endangered, and is the Government cry for Moral Support to pass unheeded?

NO, NEVER!

Are the great moral victories of Aughnacloy, Dungannon, Derry, Rosslea and Newry to be reversed at Newry?

NO, NEVER!

Unwilling as we are to engage in Political strife on the Lord's Day, we must remember that our Forefathers when Faith and Fatherland were at stake, did not hesitate because of the Sabbath, hence on an occasion like the present we have no choice but to follow their glorious example.

Assemble then, Brethren and Friends, in your strength, peacefully, calmly, and quietly, and concentrate in the Frontier Town of the Imperial Province, to loyally protest against this invasion.

Remember in the hour of danger the post of duty is the place of honour.

Wear your Regalia and Colours, and bring your Standards.

We, with others of your trusted Leaders, will be present to direct and guide you.

The Constitutionalists of Down, Armagh, Antrim, Tyrone, and Fermanagh will be with you. Everything will be ready for your reception.

GOD PROTECT THE UNION!   GOD SAVE THE QUEEN!

NO SURRENDER!

(Signed),

ARTHUR HILL, County Grand Master Down.
THOMAS WARING, Deputy Grand Master Down.

NEWRY, May 28th, 1884.

8. Nationalist electoral gains spurred unionist opposition to Home Rule. This 1884 poster featured the classic unionist slogans of 'no never', and 'no surrender'. Note too the professed loyalty to Crown and Union.

The unionist response to the first two Home Rule bills anticipated their opposition in 1912 in some ways, but such comparisons must be treated with caution. Probably the most important difference was that in the 1880s, unionism was an Irish, rather than an Ulster, phenomenon. Though many of the forces that eventually encouraged the Ulsterization of unionism were already present, northern and southern unionists found that a common enemy could help to paper over a multitude of differences. This unsteady alliance was to survive until the third Home Rule crisis, when it became clear that only some Protestants could be saved from Dublin rule.

Unionist fears were temporarily set aside by the collapse of Parnellism in highly controversial and at times sordid circumstances. Parnell had been named as a co-respondent in a divorce petition lodged in 1889 by William O'Shea, the estranged husband of Parnell's long-term mistress and mother of his children. The bitterness which accompanied his subsequent ejection as Party leader, and the already-present tensions they represented, spread through nationalist Ireland like ink on blotting paper. Parnell's desperate last-ditch attempts to claw back support during the final months of his life saw him revert to some of the fierce style and language of earlier years. But this failed to vindicate his proud and arrogant stand against the Liberal Party, most of his own party, and the Catholic Church. Like the division in the early 1920s over the Anglo-Irish Treaty; the Parnellite Split fractured the broader nationalist movement and cultivated a legacy of destructive grudges, suspicions, and vendettas.

Chapter 5
The end of the Union

The first two decades of the 20th century constituted a period of momentous and unexpected change. It appeared to one observer that 'everyone was working for a cause, for practically everything was a cause'. Causes aplenty were certainly available to budding activists in this period. Ireland nurtured a variety of cliques, intrigues, and rivalries as new cultural and political groups competed for converts. Alliances and programmes were fluid, and devotees often moved freely between organizations, amassing a variety of influences and ideas and contributing to the dynamism of the period.

Yet, despite the emergence of some challengers, the Irish Party retained a firm hold over nationalist Ireland. The ascendancy of republican politics and the consequent collapse of the Party in 1918 was unthinkable in the early years of the century. The return of the Liberals in 1906 and the introduction of the third Home Rule bill in 1912 seemed to justify the Party's constitutional strategy as well as stimulating widespread confidence in the inevitability of a native parliament. At the same time, unionism was galvanized and mobilized in opposition to Home Rule.

Once again, however, Irish affairs were to be shaped still more profoundly by external rather than internal developments. The dramatic intervention of the Great War heightened already existing tensions and created a charged political environment. Shifting mentalities and political realities heightened expectancy and mistrust, creating a society tight with tension and a context for one of the most electrifying periods in the history of modern Ireland.

Politics after Parnell

The Irish Party emerged from the Parnellite Split divided and discredited, and rifts were entrenched when the Party ruptured into anti- and pro-Parnellite factions. The Lords' rejection of Gladstone's 1893 Home Rule Bill did nothing to bring the warring factions together, and likely eroded the resolve of many Liberals who viewed Home Rule as an expensive and thankless political dead end. Party reunification came slowly and painfully, and was stimulated rather more by what were perceived to be external threats than by shared interests.

The most important of these was the formation in 1898 of William O'Brien's United Irish League. O'Brien's was an agrarian movement which attempted to build on several Parnellite traditions and to encourage Party unity. It was no Land League, but it did stimulate an impressive agrarian-nationalist campaign and gave the broader constitutional movement a much-needed boost. Leading Irish MPs were suspicious of the League, but they could not ignore its rapid expansion and potential to overtake their own organization.

The reunification of the Party under the leadership of the Parnellite, John Redmond, in 1900 was also stimulated by the untenable situation in which the factions found themselves during the centenary celebrations of the 1798 rebellion. Preparations for this commemorative event were tarnished by internecine squabbling, some of which reflected Party divisions. As rival parliamentary leaders began to appear together on various platforms from which they preached the constitutional gospel – not always easy when Tone and the United Irishmen were the ostensible focus of veneration – the logic of Party reunification became even more difficult to avoid, especially when the celebrations threatened to be hijacked by advanced nationalists.

The 'New Nationalism'

Turn-of-the-century Ireland witnessed a number of episodes which, like the 1798 centenary, stirred nationalist opinion. New and often unorthodox activism reflected a radicalization of Irish politics which was to deepen into the 20th century. Such activism was strongly influenced by the Boer War. A vigorous Irish pro-Boer movement generated a Transvaal Committee and two pro-Boer brigades. Such pro-Boer sentiment was more than symbolic: it strengthened physical force ideas and helped to fashion a number of small organizations and individuals into a loose but increasingly identifiable political grouping. Many of these people served apprenticeships in a number of essentially *ad hoc* organizations, before eventually forming the nucleus of what was to become Sinn Féin.

Sinn Féin ('ourselves') emerged in 1905, the brainchild of Arthur Griffith, the radical journalist-proprietor of *United Irishman*. Griffith wished to promote nationalist unity, but saw in the Irish Party the reasons for nationalist Ireland's disarray rather than a template for its resuscitation. Deeply critical of the Liberal alliance and what he saw as the Irish Party's prostration before it, Griffith spent much of the rest of his life creating alternatives to the Redmondite project. Sinn Féin remained marginal at first, tempting few members from the ranks of the Irish Party. Given the rather eccentric profile of much of its membership and its limited appeal, it was viewed by most contemporaries as little more than a collection of cranks.

Though highly contested, offensive, and periodically inaccurate, Griffith's journalistic output marked him out as an innovative and original thinker whose attempts to construct a 'third way' between militant nationalism and constitutionalism became influential. He addressed political, cultural, and economic questions through his newspapers and in two important pamphlets – *The Resurrection of Hungary: A Parallel for Ireland* (1904) and *The Sinn Féin Policy* (1906). He advocated a number of measures, including protectionist tariffs, parliamentary abstentionism, and a dual monarchy. Griffith was a member of the IRB until 1910 and most likely remained a separatist at heart. But this did not blind him to the necessity of offering policies to a broad spectrum of opinion; this helps to explain the eclecticism of his ideas.

Some of Griffith's views, especially the dual monarchy and his non-violent stand, rendered him suspicious to some republicans, but many nonetheless saw Sinn Féin as a useful conduit for their more advanced positions. It was the very involvement of political mavericks in his organizations that characterized them as dynamic and in some ways forward-thinking. Non-conformist women and Protestants wrote for his papers and joined him in protest, and both were welcomed into his associations. This was rare; women activists in particular were rejected by the Irish Party and almost every other political organization. Despite his dour appearance, Griffith himself provided nationalist Ireland with exciting, passionate, and entertaining journalism which served as a genuine focus for a variety of seemingly incompatible political voices.

Central to all Griffith's work and political activity was the notion that Ireland should look within itself, to its own people, resources, and traditions, for self-respect and autonomy. His emphasis on economic autarky and self-help were deeply influenced by the Irish cultural revival, another crucial force which left an indelible mark on Ireland in this period. Griffith in fact did more than any politician of his generation to politicize this ostensibly cultural movement.

The Irish cultural revival offered its mainly Catholic supporters an enthusiasm that was socially congenial and heavy in political and intellectual potential. Irish-Irelanders devoted themselves to the study and preservation of the Irish language, animated by what they perceived to be the wholesale Anglicization of Ireland. This movement mirrored similar developments on the Continent, where interest in native cultures also captured the attention of modern, middle-class urbanites. Like its European counterpart, the Irish movement was profoundly modern, relying for its success on the spread of literacy, communications, and social mobility.

Established in 1893, the Gaelic League spearheaded this interest in native culture, its founders hoping that it would serve a wide constituency, regardless of confessional or political affiliations. But as the notion of 'authentic Irishness' became sharply contested and more closely identified with Catholicism and nationalism, the League's more political members became increasingly focused on the national question and on accentuating the relationship between national identity and national independence. For expanding numbers of revivalists, the two became virtually indivisible, elevating the Irish language to a central position in the hierarchy of nationalist aspirations. A triad of Gaelicism, Catholicism, and Anglophobia formed the foundation of an exclusive, parochial, and increasingly prescriptive variety of national identity, adding to an already volatile environment.

Home Rule revived and denied

It was not to be Sinn Féin, the Gaelic League, nor the rapidly reorganizing and reviving IRB that most seriously threatened the enactment of Home Rule: unionist resistance proved to be the most serious stumbling block to the introduction of the 1912 bill, the most promising to date. The run-up to the bill had been rocky. The Liberal landslide at the 1906 general election did not immediately bring about the hoped-for legislation. Nationalist insistence could not force the Liberals into granting a concession for which they had lost their appetite. But a constitutional crisis could, and the drama which began with the 'People's Budget' in 1909 brought the possibility of Irish self-rule tantalizingly near.

The Liberals' showdown with the House of Lords led to two general elections in 1910 which left them with a reduced number of seats and in need of Labour and Irish nationalist support. This they duly got, but in exchange they pledged to introduce a third Home Rule bill, a goal whose success was made possible by the removal of the Lords' veto in 1911. The Liberals could and did present this as an opportunity to pay a long overdue debt to nationalists, and some no doubt believed that the time was right for such a bold step. But unionists, both in Ireland and within the British Conservative Party, saw it as an opportunistic and undemocratic measure, arguing that the 'nation' had not judged on the matter. There was an undeniable logic to their argument if one defined the nation as the United Kingdom, but a similar logic underpinned the nationalist claim that the Irish 'nation' had in fact spoken. The legitimacy of each position depended, of course, on which nation was said to have pronounced and which one had the moral and political right to over-ride the other.

The unionist response was swift and resolute, building on a number of existing institutions and initiatives and creating several new ones. Militancy formed a crucial part of this agenda and was evident from about 1910, confirmed by the formation of the Ulster Volunteer Force (UVF) in 1913, a paramilitary organization established to resist Home Rule by violent means if necessary. By 1912, Irish unionism had clearly become Ulster-based and focused, notwithstanding the leadership of the Dublin-born lawyer Edward Carson. Its major political institution – the Ulster Unionist Council, founded in 1905 – reflected this shift. Unionists had come to realize that they could not hope to block Home Rule for the whole island, and some began to espouse the partition of some or all of the Ulster counties as at least a partial reprieve. Though Redmond rejected the idea of permanent partition until 1916, the logic of such a settlement seemed increasingly insurmountable.

Talk of the 'Irish nation', the 'Irish people', and the 'natural and historical rights' of both had proved to be popular rallying cries for

9. A 1912 unionist postcard emphasizing unionist panic at the potential loss of economic and political ties with the United Kingdom. Note also the distinctions it draws between Ulster and the rest of Ireland.

nationalists, but unionist opposition should have forced nationalists to reconsider some of their assumptions. Instead, most nationalists fundamentally misjudged the depth of Ulster resistance and refused to admit the force of the persistent social, political, and cultural chasms between north and south. The Liberal Party was guilty of a similar misjudgement when it introduced its 1912 Bill with little consideration of unionist objections.

Why did unionists oppose Home Rule? A number of economic and political reasons were offered, including the desire to maintain links with the Empire, loyalty to the Crown and the Constitution, and, for some, a sense of Britishness which was not necessarily incompatible with Irishness. Underlining all of these was the conviction that Home Rule equalled Rome Rule and that Irish nationalism was fundamentally a Catholic edifice which had little to offer Protestants. John Redmond was unusual in reassuring unionists that their rights and influence would be safeguarded under a Dublin government. But though well-meaning, he missed the point:

unionists did not want special treatment in a Home Rule Ireland, they wanted no part in it at all; and in Ulster such sanctuary seemed feasible.

Militancy

The Ulster Volunteer Force attracted about 90,000 members. It proved effective, determined, and disciplined, evidenced by its audacious importation and distribution in 1914 of over 20,000 service rifles and 3 million rounds of ammunition, landed at Larne in one famed arms shipment. At the same time, Carson declared his willingness to preside over a provisional government. The potential for confrontation increased as high political manoeuvring failed to find a solution to the impasse over Home Rule.

The UVF's success and seeming immunity from official censure inspired a nationalist imitator in the Irish Volunteers, established in 1913 to protect the Home Rule Bill. This militia's provisional committee had strong links with the IRB, alarming Redmond and compelling him to assert some control over the burgeoning organization. The involvement of the Irish Party stimulated recruitment; membership was estimated to be over 190,000 by the end of 1914. Though never as well armed or organized as the UVF, the Volunteers nonetheless engaged in their own drilling and daring gun-running, which inspired the militarization of large sections of Catholic Ireland.

A further armed force emerged in 1913, a product of the radicalization of Irish workers. Growing trade union membership and a series of strikes and lockouts in 1912–13 raised the political temperature and the determination of employers to break the unions. The Irish Citizen Army was founded to protect workers from the brutality of the Dublin Metropolitan Police during the ferocious Dublin Lockout of 1913–14. Its membership dwindled to about 200, but it was revived by the dynamic socialist and trade union leader, James Connolly.

Like the Volunteers and the UVF, the Citizen Army drilled, adopted uniforms, and maintained a staunch commitment to military action if necessary, in its case in pursuit of a workers' republic. Fiercely opposed to the war, it claimed to serve 'neither King, nor Kaiser, but Ireland', this motto no doubt helping to build bridges between itself and the militant republicans who were in 1914 beginning to make plans for an insurrection. Connolly himself participated in talks about a proposed rising. His dream of a workers' republic was hardly shared by most of the Fenians with whom he began to conspire, but an agreement on a republic was enough to warrant cooperation: socialism, it apparently seemed to him, would follow in the wake of national independence.

The women's suffrage movement

The Irish women's movement also contributed to the general instability of this period. Like its British counterpart, the Irish suffrage movement was split along militant and non-militant lines. Unlike the British movement, however, Ireland's was also split along broadly religious lines which corresponded with the larger unionist and nationalist schism. There were attempts to bridge some of these crippling divisions, but earnest attempts to unite diverse women could not budge organizations like the Irish Women's Franchise League and the Conservative and Unionist Women's Suffrage Association.

These demarcations were unsurprisingly intensified by the Home Rule crisis, which introduced a new set of prickly considerations into the equation. Even staunch nationalist-feminists were accused of being pro-British because they lobbied the British government and assumed that women would be enfranchised under Home Rule. Such accusations were typically levied by the republican women who allied themselves with male separatist groups and sometimes formed their own auxiliary groups: they were to play a significant, though largely auxiliary, role in militant republican and socialist politics.

The spectacle of women taking to the streets, waving placards, even donning uniforms shocked some onlookers. But some women were invigorated by this activism, believing that women's rights might form part of a broader liberal political settlement in the new Ireland. The rhetoric of some of their male allies seemed to support their hopes, but the expectations raised by the temporary alliances which arose in times of crisis and extreme necessity were to be dashed in post-revolutionary Ireland.

The First World War

The government's dithering over partition and seeming inability to construct an effective Irish strategy heightened tensions. More ominously, there was genuine concern that the army would fragment over the crisis as some officers had expressed serious reservations about moving against the UVF if called upon to do so. Ensuing talks failed to break the deadlock. It is difficult to imagine how further confrontation and perhaps even civil war could have been avoided had the Great War not broken out.

The First World War was the single most important influence on the political development of modern Ireland. Its immediate effect was to diffuse internal tensions as continental hostilities were naturally given priority: the Home Rule Bill was suspended until the end of hostilities. Redmond and Carson vied to express their loyalty to the Empire by pledging Irish recruits and support for the war effort. Carson could depend on the unionist community to support his aims. Redmond, on the other hand, enjoyed a good deal of support for his stand at first, but this was increasingly eroded by a number of internal and peripheral circumstances. The first blow was the split in the Volunteer movement. The vast majority of the organization supported Redmond, while a small but determined group – infiltrated by the IRB and retaining most of the Volunteers' weaponry – mounted a concerted campaign against Irish enlistment.

10. A 1912 title page of the feminist weekly *Irish Citizen*, featuring a number of the movement's leading lights. Note the attempt at pluralism and joint action.

Redmond's support for the allied war effort was, in the context of his broader political position, perfectly logical. Participation in the (hopefully brief) war offered a number of potential benefits: Home Rule in reward for loyalty and a chance to make common cause with unionists, and in the process to convince them of nationalist dedication to the Empire. Redmond was himself a dedicated imperialist and, like many Europeans, was genuinely horrified by German atrocities. The war also stimulated the rhetoric of the rights of small nations and there were obvious Irish parallels: Belgium was not only small, it was Catholic too. Over 200,000 Irishmen volunteered for the British Army, partly in response to politicians' rallying cries, but also because of a shared condemnation of German aggression.

An unsympathetic War Office did little to support Redmond's position, but although the machinery of his Party inevitably suffered during the war, and the optimistic mood of 1912 seemed an eternity away, the constitutionalists continued to maintain a hold over nationalist Ireland until at least 1916. At the same time, the Great War accelerated militarism and provided separatists in the Volunteers, the IRB, and its own shadowy Military Council with a sense of urgency and purpose. The separatist aphorism 'England's difficulty is Ireland's opportunity' seemed more relevant than ever. Though deeply divided among themselves about the efficacy and potential success of any strike against British rule, plans were considered and a series of complicated and secret negotiations finally led to a decision to revolt at Easter 1916.

The Easter Rising

About 1,300 Irish Volunteers and 219 members of the Citizen Army turned out on Easter Monday. They seized a number of buildings around Dublin, most famously the General Post Office which housed most of the Rising's leaders. A provisional government was assembled and Patrick Pearse, as 'president', emerged from the building to read the proclamation of the Provisional Government

11. A 1915 poster issued by the Central Council for the Organization of Recruiting in Ireland. The *Lusitania* was torpedoed by a German U-boat in Irish waters.

of Ireland to a largely uncomprehending audience. The dispatch of troops to quash the Rising resulted in fierce artillery bombardment and devastating exchanges of fire.

The Easter Rising lasted less than a week. About 450 people were killed and over 2,500 were injured in the fighting between the outnumbered rebels and British forces: the majority of casualties were civilians. Whether the planners ever believed that they could achieve a military success is still open to debate, but any such hope of victory became impossible after the failure of a planned landing of German guns and the non-participation of the provincial Volunteer units, who were confused by the mixed orders issued before the Rising. This of course begs the much-asked question of why the insurgents went ahead, given that the odds were stacked so decisively against them. Explanations include the desire to inflict maximum damage in the time-honoured Fenian tradition, the hope of inciting Irish people into revolt against the Irish Party and its imperialist masters, and the related belief in the principle of action as propaganda.

The motives of individual rebels were undoubtedly mixed, but military success was neither imperative nor likely on Easter Monday. The Rising was inspired by the bloody excesses of the European war, and the war itself provided an irresistible context for its occurrence. The belligerence of the UVF, the weapons circulating through Ireland, and the prospect, still possible in 1916, that Britain might be defeated by the Germans at any time, motivated an assortment of poets, extremists, Gaelic enthusiasts, and hangers-on. Pearse himself supplied a forceful rationale at his court-martial: 'We seem to have lost. We have not lost. To refuse to fight would have been to lose; to fight is to win. We have kept the faith with the past, and handed on a tradition to the future.'

The Easter Rising and the subsequent radicalization of Irish politics were not, however, a natural culmination of over a century of republican struggle. The Rising certainly carried on a tradition, but

12. The devastation of Dublin in the aftermath of the Easter Rising. To many, such scenes were uncannily reminiscent of the destruction of parts of Belgium and France.

this was a tradition of disdain for a democratic mandate, popular support, and hope of success. But Pearse's linking of the Easter Rising to a longer trajectory of violent resistance to British rule and his articulation of a sacrosanct rationale for taking up arms proved powerful and provided his political heirs with a compelling and legitimizing sense of historical continuity.

The aftermath of the Easter Rising

Public reaction to the Rising was probably more mixed than some historians have allowed, but it could by no means be described as popular. The Rising came as a complete surprise to startled Dubliners, many of whom viewed it as a 'stab in the back' of their husbands and sons who were risking their lives in Europe. The destruction, inconvenience, and looting it triggered did little to endear the rebels to an Irish public that had placed its faith in constitutional politics.

It was, in fact, the British government that set off a change in public opinion and the elevation of the rebels to martyr status. Martial law was introduced throughout Ireland, inconveniencing people who had had no time for the rebels but who became increasingly furious at what looked very much like communal punishment. Fifteen of the rebels were shot with little heed for the consequences of this swift action. About 3,500 'suspects' were arrested, but 1,500 were speedily released, reflecting the ill-conceived nature of the operation. The internment of a further 1,841 under rather relaxed prison conditions merely allowed the detainees a useful opportunity to consolidate and prepare future strategy.

The political response was little more astute. Lloyd George offered plainly conflicting assurances on partition to the Irish Party and the unionists, but neither he nor a 1917–18 Irish Convention (boycotted by Sinn Féin and Labour) managed to forge a mutually agreeable resolution to the partition question. In the meantime, advanced nationalist opposition to the Irish Party strengthened. The Rising had bequeathed no real political strategy or even leadership, and certainly no obvious way forward, but a combination of survivors of the Rising, Gaelic enthusiasts, and other political mavericks laid the foundations for a new and formidable political movement. Though hardly coherent, Sinn Féin emerged as the focus for a number of these nationalist clusters, and the yoking of the Volunteers to Sinn Féin proved to be especially important.

Sinn Féin's anti-Redmond, anti-enlistment stand and the imprisonment of some of its members after the Rising endowed the organization with the necessary radical kudos. Crucially, however, Sinn Féin's strategy was constitutional and non-violent, rather than conspiratorial and belligerent. It challenged the Irish Party on its own territory rather than operating from the shadowy sidelines. This approach appeared to be vindicated by four by-election victories in early 1917, most notably Eamon de Valera's at East Clare. The highest ranking survivor of the Easter Rising, de Valera's American citizenship had saved him from execution and placed him at the front of the queue of potential successors to the nationalist throne.

De Valera's authority was cemented at Sinn Féin's national convention in 1917, when he was elected president of the organization, and later of the reorganized Volunteers. It was also at that meeting that de Valera announced his vision for Ireland's political future: a republic would be sought, but once secured, 'the Irish people may by referendum freely choose their own form of government'. This was an attempt to placate both the republican and dual monarchist strands within the party. Its stand on violence remained imprecise, but this fudge probably helped to win over to the movement increasing numbers of Catholic clerics.

The 1918 Military Service Bill which was to extend conscription to Ireland delivered the final blow to the flagging Irish Party. This ludicrous proposal, which even Carson had warned the cabinet against, roused Irish popular opinion to an unprecedented level. Though the Party had always opposed conscription, the fiercest protest it could muster was walking out of parliament, a symbolic vindication of Griffith's abstentionist policy. Priests, politicians, and ordinary people joined to oppose the Bill in an enormous opposition campaign; the Bill itself was fortunately made redundant by the armistice.

Sinn Féin had played a prominent role in the opposition, the Bill having provided useful proof of many of their worst predictions about British intentions. Their fame was boosted by the arrest of most of the republican leadership for involvement in a spurious 'German plot'. The resourceful Michael Collins escaped arrest, going 'on the run' and helping to plan resistance, violent if necessary, to British coercion of Sinn Féin or the Volunteers. The abrupt end of the war encouraged different strategies, notably the courting of international support for Irish independence and, in 1918, contesting the first general election since 1910.

Sinn Féin and the Irish Party competed for the votes of an electorate that had been significantly expanded by the Representation of the People Act. Sinn Féin campaigned on an ambiguous platform which attempted to be all things to all people. It exploited Redmond's position on the war, partition, and the Easter Rising. It appealed to nationalists of all shades, promised to abstain from Westminster if elected, and made few firm pledges beyond promising to work for Ireland's freedom.

The result was an electoral triumph for Sinn Féin and nothing less than a routing of the Irish Party. Sinn Féin, aided by Labour's decision not to contest the election, took less than half the total votes in Ireland as a whole, but increased its number of seats from 7 to 73, while the Irish Party plunged from 68 to 6, maintaining a tenuous hold only in Ulster. Twenty-six Ulster Unionists were also elected, having increased their share of the vote. Both unionists and nationalists had sent a very clear message to Westminster about the demands of their constituents, but these demands remained dangerously incompatible.

The Anglo-Irish War

In accordance with party policy, Sinn Féin did not take up its seats at Westminster, instead reconstituting itself in January 1919 as Dáil Éireann (the parliament of Ireland) and declaring Irish independence. De Valera, president of the Dáil and thus the Republic, embarked in April on an American tour which kept him away for 18 months. The Dáil was proscribed in August, but managed to nurture a highly successful quasi-state apparatus which disrupted and delegitimized the British dispensation at local government, judicial, and administrative levels.

Sporadic clashes between Volunteers and policemen had occurred in 1918, but the first manifest engagement in the Anglo-Irish War was the murder at Soloheadbeg, County Tipperary, of two members of the Royal Irish Constabulary (RIC) in January 1919. Some Volunteer units began to call themselves the Irish Republican Army (IRA), but coordination remained patchy as individual units staged uncoordinated raids on policemen and barracks as well as burning big houses and harassing public officials.

Stringent legislation forced many Volunteers to go 'on the run' and encouraged the formation of 'active service units' which undertook more ambitious raids. Some of these men formed 'flying columns', cadres which relied heavily on local communities to hide them as they moved from house to house, evading arrest. They staged some of the most spectacular and violent ambushes of the conflict, often defying the desperate efforts of central command to impose order on the army as a whole. At the same time, Michael Collins organized his deadly 'Squad' to systematically assassinate prominent security personnel and civil servants.

The government pursued an ever more coercive policy in response to the disruptiveness of the Volunteers, but the police could not cope with what was effectively a guerrilla war. Extra forces were recruited to try to bring the country under control,

the most notorious being the 'Black and Tans' who were sent
in to reinforce the beleaguered police, and the Auxiliaries, a
force of about 2,300 former officers. These supplementary
forces displayed a woeful degree of indiscipline, and some
engaged in felonious behaviour including arson, looting, and
murder. A vicious circle of retribution also developed, provoking
some horrendous 'retaliations' which cost innocent lives.
Estimates vary, but at least 1,200 people died during the conflict.
Public opinion was outraged, not least in Britain where the
government was coming under increasing pressure to restrain
its forces.

The ability of the Dáil and the IRA to disrupt the normal
functioning of the country and to defy British authority helped to
win the support of the Irish nationalist population, much of which
was tired of living in a virtual war zone. The country experienced
the conflict unevenly, some areas hardly being affected at all, but
moderate opinion in Britain and in Ireland was increasingly vocal
in its demand for an end to the hostilities. Both sides approached
the idea of a truce with caution. Collins knew that the IRA could not
hold out much longer, but did not want to admit this publicly, while
the British baulked at the idea of negotiating with terrorists as
though they were statesmen representing a legitimate power. A
truce which was to commence in July 1921 was, however, finally
agreed.

The truce seemed increasingly necessary in the wake of the May
elections under the Government of Ireland Act. This created two
Irish states: 26 counties under Dublin and six under Belfast. The
Belfast parliament went about the business of government briskly
(see Chapter 7), while Sinn Féin boycotted the Dublin assembly,
using the occasion to return 124 unopposed members to the
Second Dáil, convened in August 1921. A paltry four unionists were
returned to the Dublin parliament established under the Act. This
legislation failed as a conciliatory gesture: simple Home Rule was
clearly no longer acceptable to the nationalist Irish electorate, but

a compromise had to be found if further bloodshed was to be avoided.

The Anglo-Irish Treaty

A tortuous series of negotiations preceded the signing of the Anglo-Irish Treaty in December 1921. These deliberations, and the subsequent republican split over the Treaty, represent one of the most controversial and dramatic events in modern Irish history. De Valera initially rejected Lloyd George's offer of dominion status on the Canadian model with some safeguards in defence and security. But, by agreeing to negotiations proper from September, Sinn Féin implicitly agreed to negotiate on the basis of 26 county dominion status: anything more than this was going to be very difficult to achieve.

To the astonishment of many and the continuing perplexity of historians, de Valera, having been recently and defiantly named President of the Irish Republic, remained at home. The Irish plenipotentiaries were led by Collins and Griffith, both pragmatists who commanded significant authority within Sinn Féin. They represented a party which remained divided on the issue of a minimum level of independence, and so had no absolute idea of what would prove to be acceptable to a majority. The issue of partition was effectively shelved, both sides agreeing in principle to partition but not to the border, which would be considered at a later date.

Under considerable pressure, the delegates signed the 'Articles of an Agreement for a Treaty between Great Britain and Ireland' on 6 December. This wording suggested sovereignty, and the adoption of 'Irish Free State' placated some nationalists, though die-hard republicans were enraged at the dropping of 'Republic'. A political status that allowed for far more autonomy than Home Rule had ever promised was achieved, though some fiscal and military conditions were attached. The ostensible sticking point was the continuing connection with the British Empire and the abandonment of Irish autonomy represented by Lloyd George's insistence on an oath of fidelity to the monarch and the Commonwealth.

The Irish public appeared to support the Treaty, or at least to support an agreement which guaranteed the cessation of hostilities. But within the Dáil, obdurate delegates denounced the signatories as 'traitors' to the 'republican ideal'. Griffith and Collins insisted that it was the best available compromise and that there was no alternative but a renewed Anglo-Irish war which the Irish could not win. Collins memorably argued that the Treaty 'gives us freedom – not the ultimate freedom that all nations desire and develop to, but the freedom to achieve it', but his eloquent plea fell on many deaf ears.

Partition remained a side issue during the Treaty debates. In common with Griffith and Collins, many firmly believed that partition was a temporary measure and that Northern Ireland would fail to function as a viable economic unit, thus inducing unification. The convoluted, passionate, and sometimes pedantic views exchanged by pro- and anti-Treaty delegates exposed broader ideological discord which had been kept at bay by unified opposition to the British. This shaky unity collapsed quickly under the strain of the Treaty debates.

Chapter 6
Independent Ireland

What one nationalist described as nationalist Ireland's 'desperate homesickness for a Split' once again reared its ugly head in the aftermath of the vote on the Anglo-Irish Treaty. In January 1922, Dáil Éireann delivered its verdict: 64 votes for, and 57 against. The ballot itself was hardly a ringing endorsement of the settlement, but it did reflect general nationalist opinion in the country, if not in the Dáil. The hard-fought battle over the Treaty's ratification instilled in its pragmatic advocates a determination to defend it against all comers. It also shaped the divisions which were to characterize Irish politics for decades. The first ostensible break became obvious when de Valera led his followers out of the Dáil after the Treaty's confirmation. Ireland was once again polarized and plunged into crisis. It was to be the first of many challenges to the new state.

The Treaty and Civil War

Michael Collins became chairman of the provisional government formed a week after the Treaty debate. Any hope of an easy transition to normal politics was dashed by the dissenting anti-Treaty minority, famously described by Kevin O'Higgins, Minister for Justice, as 'wild men screaming through the keyhole'. The animosity between pro- and anti-Treaty Sinn Féin was indeed savage, and deeply destabilizing as both sides anxiously set about to capture the loyalty of the potentially pivotal IRA: Collins's supporters within the organization constituted the basis of what was to become the Free State Army, while anti-Treaty IRA members became known as 'Irregulars'. In April, the latter took up positions in the Four Courts and other significant and symbolically important buildings in Dublin. Despite soothing words and initiatives suggested by both sides, armed conflict looked increasingly likely.

Public opinion endorsed the Treaty at a general election held in June. The anti-Treatyites won 36 of a total of 128 seats, while pro-Treaty Sinn Féin took 58. The rest went to Labour (17), the Farmers' Party (7), and independents (10), all of which supported the Treaty. Voters' motives were no doubt mixed: the desire for peace probably motivated more constituents than ideological considerations, but an unquestionable majority had spoken. A public mandate was not, however, enough to convince the dissidents, who remained entrenched in the Four Courts. Having refused an order to evacuate, the Provisional Government's troops fired upon the Irregulars on 28 June. A vicious war between former fellow soldiers and friends thus began in Dublin, before moving to other cities and towns and ending in a miserable series of guerrilla-like ambushes and skirmishes.

The Civil War lasted from June until the following May. The final death toll remains uncertain: the government claimed that 800 of its forces had been killed, but the republican death toll was higher. Anti-Treaty forces had not been able to capitalize on their initial military advantage and, perhaps more significantly, had not won popular support for their stand. The backing of the Catholic hierarchy added legitimacy to the Provisional Government. The insurgents who maintained their fight against the democratically elected government faced excommunication.

Legitimately elected it certainly was, but the Provisional Government's standing was called into question during the conflict. It sanctioned ruthless and at times brutal actions which highlighted the grim reality of war between former comrades, executing

77 Irregulars and interning over 10,000 people without trial, inevitably provoking unedifying parallels between its behaviour and the British government's during the Anglo-Irish War.

The Irish Free State

The legacy of the Civil War, the death and carnage, the material destruction, and the schisms it had amplified scarred Ireland for several decades, and deprived it of some its most able leaders, including Michael Collins, who had been killed in an ambush in August 1922. The pro-Treaty party was repackaged in May 1923 as Cumann na nGaedheal (the name of one of Griffith's earliest groupings). The anti-Treatyites retained the name Sinn Féin and that party's traditional abstentionist stand until they too split in 1926. In the immediate aftermath of the Civil War, however, Ireland was effectively a one-party state as Sinn Féin refused to sit in the new lower house, maintaining instead a stubborn loyalty to the Second Dáil of 1921. Only Labour provided some kind of opposition.

The priorities of the fledgling government were order and stability. The Provisional Government had made significant inroads by founding an unarmed police force, Gárda Síochána, and constructing a democratic political system through the constitution of 1922. Cumann na nGaedheal built on this, establishing a record of solid though unimaginative administration which neglected – or ditched – several opportunities for innovation. The country's legal and political systems retained a solidly British flavour: continuity rather than innovation was to characterize the new administration.

Despite significant achievements, notably in boosting the new State's international status, a sense of disappointment pervades most accounts of the early years of the Irish Free State. Cumann na nGaedheal governed effectively during a difficult time, but it did so without exhibiting much flair or charisma. This, coupled with its own failure to cultivate crucial grass roots support, damaged public perceptions of its electability. The party also earned a damaging reputation for miserliness by cutting pensions and salaries and fostering economic alarmism. One imprudent minister famously announced in 1924 that 'people may have to die in the country and die through starvation'. This was hardly music to the ears of electors.

Probably more fatal was the fact that the State's first politicians had tried to build on a settlement which could not disguise the incompleteness of the Irish revolution. The republican aims and aspirations of a number of constituencies that had guided Irish resistance to British rule were simply not realized under the terms of the Anglo-Irish Treaty. Patience with Collins's stepping-stone approach to Irish freedom was wearing thin, and suspicion grew that some ministers viewed the Treaty as a final rather than an interim settlement.

North-South relations

The Boundary Commission confirmed the worst of these gloomy suspicions. The Commission finally met in 1924, sitting pointlessly through most of the following year. The Free State's representative, Eoin MacNeill, resigned after a controversial leak to the press late in 1925. A formal report was not issued, and an agreement was struck instead between the three governments. In the end, the existing arrangements were enforced and the status of the Treaty as a conduit for nationalist objectives plummeted still further.

This, more than any of the many difficulties faced by the Cumann na nGaedheal government, underlined the partial nature of the revolution. It is, however, difficult to see how the outcome could have been any different. The Government of Ireland Act had allowed for Northern Ireland to opt out of the Irish Free State, and there is precious little evidence to suggest that unionists were minded to forfeit this opportunity. The Northern government in fact exercised this right in March 1922. The Boundary Commission represented the last opportunity to overturn partition short of military action: its failure to do this was an embarrassing disappointment for the government and a propaganda gift to its vindicated enemies.

The prospects for Irish reunification were very faint indeed in the early 1920s, but possibilities for fostering better relations between North and South did exist, especially through the initially promising Craig–Collins pacts of 1922. These came to very little. Collins, hopeful that the forthcoming Boundary Commission would end partition, had presided over the Provisional Government's 'non-recognition' policy of Northern Ireland. At the same time, he supported the northern IRA and applied political pressure to the Belfast government. One Irish statesman described this belligerent approach in the iciest of terms: 'under the terms of the treaty we recognize the [Northern] parliament in order to destroy it'.

This confrontational policy was, however, to be whittled down during the Civil War. The Free State government had little appetite for further military adventure and had no wish to jeopardize the terms of the Treaty. Despite real concerns for the plight of Northern Catholics, a consensual approach to (eventual) unification emerged in tandem with the realization that the Dublin government could do little to affect the treatment of its Northern brethren.

The normalization of Irish politics

Irish politics settled into a more recognizably democratic form when de Valera founded the Fianna Fáil party and began to steer it towards the Dáil. He had hinted at such a course since 1923, and in 1926 he provoked another Sinn Féin split by claiming that he might enter the Dáil if the oath of allegiance were removed. The new party's aims repudiated many of the values and constituencies that Cumann na nGaedheal was seen to uphold. It championed traditional republican aspirations about the fundamental unity of the country and built up a populist programme which contrasted sharply with the austere and unexciting policies pursued by Cumann na nGaedheal. It also emitted a whiff of its erstwhile extremism, a leading gunman turned politician describing it as a 'slightly constitutional' party.

Fianna Fáil won 44 seats to Cumann na nGaedheal's 47 at the 1927 general election, confirming de Valera's belief that his party faced a promising electoral future. Its final move into parliamentary politics was facilitated by the government's Electoral Amendment Bill, which effectively rendered abstention illegal. This rather extraordinary (masochistic, some have argued) measure stimulated the democratic process by forcing opposition candidates to take the oath, or to cease to stand for election altogether.

Under de Valera, Fianna Fáil began its phenomenal rise to power. Having entered the Dáil – and treated the oath in the same dismissive manner which his critics had urged on him in 1922 – he developed strong constituency organizations, especially in rural Ireland, and effective propaganda organs. Fianna Fáil's populist-nationalist rhetoric evidently struck a chord. Though reliant on Labour for its majority after the 1932 election, a snap election called the following year saw it win an overall majority, while Cumann na nGaedheal's fortunes slumped still further.

Fianna Fáil in power: extremism

Political extremists – on the right and the left of Irish politics – posed the most formidable immediate challenges to the new government. Formed in 1931, the Army Comrades Association – renamed the National Guard in 1932, but known as the Blueshirts because of their uniform adopted in the same year – became a focus for opposition to Fianna Fáil. In 1933 the increasingly desperate Cumann na nGaedheal joined the Centre Party and the National Guard to form Fine Gael, a motley crew which presented itself as an alliance against an imagined 'red scare'. Tensions mounted as street violence between the Blueshirts and the IRA marred the 1933 election campaign, and sporadic clashes continued. De Valera responded decisively, and by 1934 the Blueshirts had effectively been routed.

Though no doubt influenced by continental fascism, the Blueshirts in reality offered little more than a pale imitation of the German, Spanish, and Italian varieties. The organization gathered backing, but it never managed to galvanize widespread ideological commitment to its murky variety of fascism. The same may be said for the IRA, which posed another threat to the government. Its leftwing offshoot, Saor Éire, was short-lived and had little chance of thriving in staunchly anti-communist Catholic Ireland. De Valera lifted restrictions against the IRA, but he used the hated Public Safety Act against it and the Blueshirts. In 1936 he re-banned the IRA in response to a spate of murders. Further uncompromising anti-IRA measures followed. Under the Emergency Powers Act of 1940, hundreds of IRA prisoners were interned without trial: some were executed, while others were permitted to die while on hunger strike. Like his pro-Treaty enemies before him, de Valera was unwilling to countenance any threat to his State, notwithstanding shared aspirations and earlier solidarity.

Irish sovereignty

On a legislative level, Fianna Fáil enhanced significantly Ireland's self-determination and freedom of action. Removing the remnants of British rule began with 1933's Constitutional Amendment (Removal of Oath) Bill. Two additional acts – the Irish Nationality and Citizenship Act and the Aliens Act – defined anyone who was not a citizen of the Irish Free State as an alien: pointedly, this included British subjects.

The Anglo-Irish agreement of 1938 was the most important legislation in this area. It stabilized relations between the states after several acrimonious exchanges. De Valera himself saw the accomplishment of this settlement as a great political success, and it did indeed win important concessions for Ireland at a very low cost. The land annuities question was settled once and for all through a final Irish payment of ten million pounds (seen by most historians as a bargain). Ireland also achieved the return of the 'Treaty ports', administered by the British under the Anglo-Irish Treaty. These, along with de Valera's cultivation of an international profile, were to provide a crucial foundation for Ireland's neutrality during the Second World War.

De Valera also entertained real hopes – or at least proclaimed in public that he did – of a united Ireland. His party's policy was certainly not an aggressive one in the military sense. The Free State had no feasible hope of sustaining a military campaign against the Belfast government, even if the will had existed. De Valera expressed the idea that only good government in the 'twenty-six counties' might tempt the majority in Northern Ireland to accept a united Ireland. But, to the indignation of Northern unionists, he continued to articulate the aspiration, indeed the moral imperative, of unification.

The 1937 constitution

This was nowhere better and more simply expressed than in articles two and three of the 1937 constitution – Bunreacht na hÉireann. Article two claimed 'the national territory consists of the whole island of Ireland', and article three stated that the constitution would only apply to the 26 counties 'pending the reintegration of the national territory'. The constitution reflected the Catholic tenor of the country. Composed almost entirely by de Valera himself and the product of two years' hard work and consultation, it rendered Ireland a republic in all but name. The word 'republic' was not used, perhaps because it might have offended unionist sensibilities, but more likely because a 26-county state did not represent the Ireland of republican aspirations.

The constitution established Irish as the country's first language

(English received recognition as second official language), replaced the governor-generalship with a presidency, and changed the country's name to Éire. The prime minister was henceforth to be known as the Taoiseach, and the senate (abolished in 1936) was reconstituted as a vocationally selected body with diluted powers. The only major opposition was raised by feminists, who were particularly concerned with article 41.2 as its clauses emphasized women's 'life within the home' and outlined the state's aim to 'ensure that mothers shall not be obliged by economic necessity to engage in labour to the neglect of their duties in the home'.

One female columnist described the constitution as the 'death knell of the working woman', but in reality these clauses reflected rather than defined broader social attitudes to the family, and added to the work already being done by complementary legislation. However, the symbolic importance of these clauses was not lost on many stalwarts of the feminist movement (sneeringly described by one journalist as 'Women Graduates Again'), who very much viewed them as an attack on independent, unmarried, and professional women. Other critics, especially those associated with the women's labour movement, bemoaned the fact that the government did nothing in reality to improve the lot of mothers by, for example, increasing men's wages so that married women would not be forced to seek paid employment. De Valera himself dismissed criticism, declaring rather defensively in the Dáil, 'I seem to have got a bad reputation. I do not think I deserve it'. Many disagreed.

The Emergency

Ireland remained neutral during the Second World War, or 'the Emergency' as it was officially known, though in reality the country's neutrality was pro-Allied. Certain military privileges were allowed the Allies, and different treatment was meted out to the German and Allied prisoners of war who were captured in Irish territory. This may have been a product of both design and accident, but the crucial point was that Ireland dictated its own policy during a critical period of international crisis – independently of Britain.

A number of strategic reasons may be offered to explain Ireland's neutral stand: the possibility of a German victory was very real, indeed likely at times, thus an alliance with the Allies might have made Ireland's post-war prospects more difficult; Ireland could have mounted only token resistance to a German invasion at the potential cost of the battering of its cities (of the kind Belfast endured); and Ireland had no quarrel with Germany. But neutrality in fact allowed Ireland to have its cake and eat it too. Numbers are uncertain, but up to 50,000 Irish citizens joined the Allied war effort and many thousands more took war-linked jobs in Britain. Pro-allied opinion was strong. Ireland probably felt that it had a chance of British protection in any case, given that a German invasion of the island would have severely jeopardized Britain's own security.

British statesmen were in fact so desperate to get Ireland on side that first Chamberlain in 1940 and then Churchill in 1941 suggested the possibility of Irish unity in exchange for the end of neutrality. Both offers were rejected: neither offered anything substantial, and neutrality was a popular policy which carried great symbolic value. The Irish population felt the impact of war through shortages, rationing, and draconian censorship which hindered informed discussion about the war. Neutrality itself was certainly taken too far when, on the death of Hitler, de Valera presented the state's condolences to the German legation. No other neutral state made such a tactless gesture.

Crucially, neutrality allowed Ireland a kind of moral victory: it had held firm, resisted the appeals of Britain and America, and had come through the war virtually unscathed. But this 'victory' relied on the fact that Ireland had escaped the brutality experienced by so many other small European nations which similarly had had no quarrel with Germany.

The Irish economy

Cumann na nGaedheal's economic policy had been a product of necessity, a lack of imagination, and dependence on British norms. The Irish pound continued to exchange on a par with sterling, and the Department of Finance kept a tight grip on economic policy, developing an almost obsessive dedication to balanced budgets and frugality. It was guided by the arguments presented in 1923 by a Fiscal Inquiry Committee which pronounced against the republican holy grail of protective tariffs.

But older assumptions about the appropriate shape of Ireland's economy persisted. According to the 1926 census, 53% of Ireland's workforce was employed in agriculture, although the actual rate was likely higher as farmers' wives were not included in this figure. But the prospects for Irish agriculture were not bright in the early 1920s as the privileged position Irish farmers had enjoyed as suppliers to Britain during the Great War had been eroded in the post-war slump. The government set in place a number of measures to improve Irish produce, and some effort was put into education and training, but they were frustrated by increased competition and falling prices for agricultural produce. Over 90% of Ireland's exports went to Britain in the 1920s, but Britain was flattered by a host of potential suppliers, some of whom boasted cheaper and better quality products than Ireland.

Irish industry faced equally serious and similar problems. Competition was intense and Irish industry itself suffered through poor management and a dearth of skilled workers. There were signs of improvement by 1930, but Ireland's economy, as ever, was not immune from international trends and it was inevitably battered by the fall-out from the Wall Street Crash. The government's response was a swift increase in protective tariffs, a policy that imitated contemporary European responses to the crisis. This was maintained and in fact augmented under Fianna Fáil, which was ideologically committed in any case to economic self-sufficiency and the loosening of economic dependence on Britain.

Legislative attempts were made under the Fianna Fáil government in the early 1930s to confine industry to Irish owners, but these were not pursued with any great vigour. A new industrial drive was initiated and support given in the form of the Irish Credit Corporation. The result was a general growth in industrial activity, but this represented an increase in short-term work rather than the building up of a more stable industrial sector for the future. Fianna Fáil also subsidized many state-sponsored initiatives, including the Irish Sugar Company and Aer Lingus, as part of its self-sufficiency drive. These were innovative measures, but their success and impact on general prosperity is debatable.

One of the most important economic issues – in political and financial terms – of the period was what came to be known as the 'economic war' between Ireland and Great Britain. This was prompted by Fianna Fáil's withholding of land annuities to the British exchequer. A furious British government responded by imposing heavy duties on Irish livestock; de Valera in turn imposed duties on British coal. It is difficult to separate the financial consequences of the economic war from the political effects. Irish public opinion seemed to support de Valera's stand, though some of his colleagues were less sure. It seems, however, that with or without this impasse, sections of Ireland's economy were in any case bound to suffer in the 1930s, and there was political mileage to be gained in refusing to bow to the pressure of the British Treasury. The stalemate was settled, finally, through the Coal and Cattle Pact of 1935, but de Valera had unquestionably struck a symbolically important blow for Irish sovereignty.

Despite Fianna Fáil's dedication to Griffithite autarky and the development of a thriving rural sector in which tillage rather than livestock would dominate – the assumption being that tillage enhanced employment, thus helping to stem emigration – the rural sector simply did not thrive. In reality, the industrial share of the employment market grew, self-sufficiency was not even remotely realized, emigration in very high numbers continued, and Britain remained Ireland's biggest market by far. On the other hand, social welfare payments were increased, helping to alleviate the distress of the very poor, and the worst excesses of the worldwide depression did not bedevil Ireland. By 1940, Ireland's economic planners had not produced the rural, self-sufficient Gaelic idyll that de Valera had dreamed of, but the economy looked healthier than it had in 1932, and was a good sight more healthy than many of its shattered European counterparts.

Education and identity

Ireland's new independent status invigorated campaigns for the organization of the nation along Catholic and Gaelic lines. Education was seen to be crucial to this process, and a series of educational initiatives saw the Irish language occupy a central place in the curriculum. This process was intensified in the 1930s: Irish became a compulsory subject in secondary schools from 1934, having been introduced into primary schools in the 1920s. A competence in Irish was made compulsory for some civil service positions. Though some educationalists warned that the emphasis on Irish would lower standards in other subjects (as it probably did), this general strategy enjoyed the blessing of both main parties. Likewise, the inclusion in school curricula of a blatantly nationalist version of Irish history which more or less 'skipped the difficult bits' was tolerated.

The problem remained, however, that such an emphasis on compulsion inevitably dulled enthusiasm. This was not helped by an initial dearth of suitably qualified or interested teachers, but more corrosive still was the simple fact that few opportunities existed for Irish to be spoken outside schools. The Gaelic revival failed to make Irish a truly living language because successive governments refused to face the unpleasant reality that much broader swathes of Irish life would have to be Gaelicized if proficiency was to become both universal and enduring. It seems that the Irish population largely shared this schizophrenic view, believing the language to be central to Irish culture and identity, but doubting its suitability for contemporary life. And the necessities of contemporary life applied abroad too: as in the 19th century, Irish was no help to the thousands of Irish people who continued to emigrate to English-speaking countries.

A Catholic state?

In the late 1920s, a *Church of Ireland Gazette* editorial stated 'the undoubted fact that the Irish Free State is very predominantly a Roman Catholic country, and has become so more decidedly between 1911 and 1926'. It is not difficult to see why the *Gazette*

IRISH TRADE JOURNAL AND STATISTICAL BULLETIN

IRISleabar τráðála aγus ŗeasacán scaιτιsτιðeacτa na héιreann

VOL. XIII. No. 4.   DECEMBER, 1938   PRICE 4D.

13. An idyllic image from the *Irish Trade Journal and Statistical Journal* of 1938 which neatly encapsulated the government's idealized and outmoded view of trade, industry, and commerce.

reached this conclusion, but as Charles Townshend has recently argued, 'notions of what constituted a Catholic state inevitably differed'. The Catholic Church was not made the state church in independent Ireland, but the country's social legislation was unquestionably informed by confessional considerations. The Catholic bishops and various politicians disagreed at different times about how far legislation should reflect Catholic doctrine, but an accommodation between church and state was generally achieved. The hierarchy itself retained a formidable presence within Irish society, aided by expanding numbers of hard-working lay organizations whose own periodicals outlined Catholic social policy in the frankest of terms.

Public and private morality came under increased scrutiny and policing after independence. The almost hysterical denunciations in the 1920s and 1930s of dance halls, jazz, and immodest fashion (for women, of course) reflected broader European and North American panic about the supposed erosion of moral codes triggered by the First World War. It would thus be incorrect to claim that Irish legislation on film and literary censorship, divorce, and birth control was unparalleled – especially as Irish politicians looked very closely at foreign legalization before drawing up their own – but it would be equally absurd to fail to recognize the specificity of some of these measures, which differed from international initiatives in important ways. The most striking of these is birth control, which was banned with little or no recourse to the demographic and eugenic concerns and debates that underpinned similar legislation in continental Europe. In Ireland, moral concerns were paramount.

Restrictions on divorce and access to information about contraceptives had been introduced in the 1920s and strengthened in the following decade when the importation and sale of contraceptives was made illegal, and divorce was banned under the 1937 constitution. Some historians have interpreted as acquiescence the lack of strong and vocal opposition to these measures. Certainly, many people from various backgrounds supported such legislation and opposition was limited. But the hostile climate in which critics were forced to articulate their resistance formed a formidable barrier against open discussion of controversial issues. Ministers were on the whole careful not to provoke theological and moral disputes and did not offend the sensitivities of Protestants if they could avoid it, but a number of mainly Catholic periodicals displayed no such restraint, publishing poisonous and offensive denunciations of the recalcitrants who dared to question restrictive legislation.

The constitution's recognition of the 'special position' of the Roman Catholic Church was in some ways little more than a statement of the obvious, and it should be noted that the constitution also guaranteed religious toleration for all its citizens. It might well be true that the symbolic and real value of this clause has been exaggerated. At the same time, however, it should be remembered that Irish citizens who worshipped at non-Catholic altars, or at none, were bound by law that reflected Catholic social teaching, whether or not this conflicted with their own beliefs or those of their church.

Notwithstanding some very animated opposition to the 1929 Censorship of Publications Act, Irish Protestants largely held their tongues when such legislation was introduced. A number of prominent Southern unionists had made their peace with the Free State's government and undoubtedly saw in Cumann na nGaedheal and the Treaty it upheld a far more tolerable state of affairs than the anti-Treatyites. Protestants continued to be highly represented in the professions and in business, but their numbers declined dramatically, by one-third between 1911 and 1926. Protestant deaths in the Great War account for some of this decline, but it was also due to high levels of emigration in the early 1920s, sometimes in the face of outright intolerance and intimidation at the hands of republicans and Catholic ideologues. For a disillusioned minority, Home Rule had indeed become Rome Rule.

Chapter 7
Northern Ireland since 1922

The 1920 Government of Ireland Bill created the new state of Northern Ireland from the six northeastern Ulster counties of Londonderry, Tyrone, Fermanagh, Antrim, Down, and Armagh. Not having sought a Home Rule settlement for Ulster, but recognizing it as preferable to a Dublin parliament, Unionist leader James Craig claimed as 'the supreme sacrifice' Ulster unionism's acceptance of six-county exclusion. This probably gave cold comfort to the Protestants of Monaghan, Cavan, and Donegal, who were effectively abandoned to the uncertainty of Home Rule.

Craig had rebuffed attempts to form a nine-county, all-Ulster state. In common with his southern counterparts, he set out to build a state which would contain and reflect the cultural and religious prejudices common to his part of Ireland. He sought above all to preserve Protestant authority in the new state: this meant a border which would guarantee a unionist majority. The population of the province in 1926 was 1,256,561, of whom 33.5% were Catholic, 31.3% Presbyterian, and 27% Anglican. The Protestant majority was confirmed. The Ulster Unionist Party formed every government until 1972.

The parliament, known as Stormont from 1932 when it moved to Stormont Castle outside Belfast, was in reality an elaborate system of local government, whose actions were tightly constrained by the

14. The Northern Ireland parliament was opened by George V on
22 June 1921, amidst both hope and uncertainty about the future
of the fledgling state.

relative poverty of the province. The financial aspects of the Government of Ireland Act left little room for imaginative economic initiatives, and the Belfast government was crippled by an almost consistently poor economy and associated high unemployment. Some attempts were made to alleviate Northern Ireland's economic woes, but on the whole Belfast governments lacked both the skill and the resources to tackle serious economic problems. The basic problem remained that Ulster could not pay its own way and thus became reliant on British government handouts and concessions.

Political violence

Political and sectarian violence destabilized the new state from the outset. Sectarian conflict, already a fact of life in the region, escalated in 1920, raising fears of a pogrom against Catholics: over 5,000 Catholic workers were expelled from Belfast shipyards that year. Eighty-two people were killed in clashes over two months; this figure rose to 428 over the next two years. Estimates of death and injury as a result of conflict vary, but almost 300 murders were officially recorded in 1922. This represented the peak of sectarian and political violence during what had effectively become a civil war.

Northern Protestants not unreasonably believed themselves to be under siege from the southern IRA, its masters in the Dáil, and its supporters in the six counties. In 1920 the Dáil initiated the 'Belfast Boycott' in an effort to cripple the northern economy and to register its abhorrence at the treatment of northern Catholics. This was later called off, but continuing IRA raids on northern targets, the murder of a unionist MP, and confrontation on the border in 1922 raised fears of invasion. A diminution of border conflict resulted from the prosecution of the civil war, but this, like the provisional government's non-recognition policy, did little to assuage unionist anxiety.

The Northern Irish government responded to this uncertainty with a series of legislative measures, most importantly the 1922 Civil Authorities (Special Powers) Act, which was introduced initially for one year, but reintroduced every year after that until it was made permanent in 1933. This draconian legislation included provision for flogging, curfew, and internment. It was used almost exclusively against the Catholic minority. This naturally incensed Catholics, who viewed it as another sinister portent of their status in the Protestant state, while Protestants largely saw it as a necessary measure in the face of civil war and continuing harassment from the South.

In addition, the UVF had begun to reconstitute itself in 1920. Its members flocked into the new Ulster Special Constabulary, whose part-time B Specials division in particular displayed a lamentable level of indiscipline and rank prejudice against Catholic suspects. The Royal Ulster Constabulary (RUC) replaced the Royal Irish Constabulary in 1922. It enjoyed an illustrious reputation among Protestants and was staunchly defended by the government. The RUC was locally recruited, very predominantly Protestant (the intention to fill one-third of the force with Catholics was never achieved), and it was implicated in some grisly sectarian killings.

This explosive situation was exacerbated by the uncertainty of the border. Though Craig's government had moved successfully to inhibit the IRA, the Boundary Commission loomed as a potential threat to the state. The outcome obviously delighted the relieved Belfast government, but left Northern Catholics disappointed and uneasy. No less than the Southern Protestants, they too were left to fend for themselves in a hostile environment.

Unionist consolidation

Northern Ireland was at once a democratic state and a bastion of Protestant power. A Protestant electoral majority was perfectly legitimate given the state's demographic profile, but very little effort was made to alleviate the polarized nature of sectarian and political allegiances. Politics were overwhelmingly shaped by the border question: the Unionist Party dedicated itself to maintaining its electoral hegemony, while nationalist resistance to partition remained unequivocal, but waned under uninterrupted unionist majority government. Emphasizing the need for Protestant solidarity in the face of the nationalist menace – both internal and external – provided a popular rallying cry for the Unionist Party, but in fact independent unionist and Labour candidates posed more of a threat to the hegemony of Craig's party than nationalists. The abolition of proportional representation for parliamentary elections in 1929 helped to shore up unionist prevalence at the expense of Labour and independents, but it also further eroded what little Catholic confidence in the state remained.

Nationalist participation in government was hindered by the abolition in 1922 of proportional representation for local elections. The accompanying redrawing of ward and divisional boundaries weakened nationalist representation in local government, even in councils with Catholic majorities. This produced some staggering results, most scandalously in Derry. In addition, a restrictive local government franchise allowed multiple voting for some and disenfranchised those who did not pay rates. More Protestants were actually disenfranchised by this, but Catholics benefited less from the business vote and were proportionally worse off under the system. This electoral anomaly was retained in Northern Ireland even after its abolition in Britain.

No coherent nationalist parliamentary opposition appeared until 1928 when the National League of the North was formed, but a burst of futile abstention followed in the early 1930s and no effective leader emerged after the death of the demagogic Joseph Devlin in 1934. But more important was the psychological adjustment to the status of a permanent, mistrusted, and seemingly ineffectual minority.

Discrimination

Prejudice in private employment, the professions, and small businesses was unquestionably widespread, building on a much longer tradition of sectarian distrust and the maintenance of separate communities in which both Catholics and Protestants were complicit. Suspicions on both sides fuelled a grievance culture in which each community believed itself to be under siege and considered a gain for the other a deliberate blow to their own community. The fact that Catholics and Protestants lived largely segregated lives both exacerbated such conceptions and ensured that there existed little chance of overcoming them. In addition, clientelism and strong regional variations made formal and informal discrimination almost inevitable and highly difficult to police, even if the will to do so had existed.

Discrimination was never as calculated as nationalists maintained, nor as fictional as unionists claimed. The truth lies somewhere in the middle, allowing both sides ample space for the construction of myths, accusations, retaliation, and a seeming inability to resist the lure of nit-picking over details which seem trivial to the outside observer but take on momentous significance in the close world of Northern Irish politics. About the only thing on which both communities agreed – and in this they were adamantly supported by their clerics – was that the barriers between them should remain rock-hard. Co-education, social interaction, and 'mixed marriages' were as uncommon as ecumenical initiatives.

John Whyte's very thorough assessment of discrimination identified inequity of varying levels in: electoral practices, public employment, policing, private employment, public housing, and regional policy. Discrimination was especially acute at the local authority level and in nationalist areas west of the Bann. Notwithstanding some variation, it is clear that Catholics remained poorer, less well educated, and more likely to be unemployed than Protestants. The difficult question remains, however, of how much Catholic disadvantage was due to active discrimination and how much to Catholics' voluntary withdrawal from the state and its functions.

Catholics were largely hostile to the state from its inception and this merely confirmed Protestant suspicions of their disloyalty. Nationalists came under pressure from their own communities not to take up positions in the RUC and in the civil service, ensuring that their representation in these spheres remained low. They developed a kind of sub-state with their own newspapers, schools, clubs, church, and recreational activities. Unionist governments did little to correct this situation, sustaining the idea that Catholics were an undesirable presence rather than fellow citizens. Very little effort was made to integrate Catholics and to rein in the Protestant character of the state, even after the IRA threat had dissipated.

Crucial too was Northern Ireland's generally weak economic situation, which enhanced competition for jobs and resources and undoubtedly augmented the informal practice of looking after one's own. Apart from the agricultural sector, the region's economy declined and the government was for the most part unable to reverse this situation. Levels of unemployment remained consistently above the United Kingdom average for Catholics and Protestants, and periods of severe economic distress often also coincided with sectarian conflict. Catholic and Protestant workers banded together in protest against harsh economic conditions in 1932, but this proved to be as unique as it was transitory: shared poverty could not overcome ancient suspicions.

Paths to reform and rebellion

Northern Ireland made a valuable economic and strategic contribution to the Allied war effort, and paid heavily for its loyalty. German bombs devastated parts of Belfast, killing 745 people in one bombing raid on the city in 1941. A small sweetener was granted by the 1949 Ireland Act which endowed Stormont, rather than the people of Northern Ireland, with the ultimate right to

15. The aftermath of a German bombing raid on Belfast.

decide the constitutional position of the state. This bestowed a sense of security and underlined the need to keep unionist unity intact.

But keeping unionism cohesive proved to be an impossible task. A combination of economic pressures, increased Catholic self-confidence, and British involvement eroded unity and ultimately led to the implosion of unionism and the collapse of Stormont. One of the major catalysts for this was the civil rights movement, which attempted to address the residual problem of Catholic disadvantage, in housing at first then in a number of other areas including local government, policing, and employment. This stimulated the establishment of a number of organizations, including the Campaign for Social Justice (CSJ) in 1964, the Northern Ireland Civil Rights Association (NICRA) in 1967, and its radical student affiliate People's Democracy (PD) in 1968.

The civil rights movement's respectability and its dedication to non-violent protest won it important allies, particularly in the British Labour Party, and this led to a spectacular mobilization of Catholic opinion by the late 1960s. The leaders of these organizations emphasized their non-sectarian credentials, but whether the bulk of their supporters shared this view is questionable. As the prominent activist Eamonn McCann asserted in 1969:

> Everyone applauds loudly when one says in a speech that we are not sectarian, we are fighting for the rights of all Irish workers, but really that's because they see this as the new way of getting at the Protestants.

Traditional republican politics adjusted to the civil rights movement, realizing that this new campaign provided a useful and much more productive focus than violent resistance. Cross-fertilization undoubtedly occurred between republicans and the broader civil rights movement, but the idea that the civil rights campaign, and especially NICRA, was little more than an IRA front is simply unsustainable. Republicans no doubt welcomed the convergence of Catholics in demonstrations, but such protest was prompted by many factors, not a grand republican strategy.

The civil rights movement was both encouraged and frustrated by the nominally reforming efforts of Terence O'Neill, Prime Minister of Northern Ireland from 1963, who attempted to 'persuade Catholics in Northern Ireland that they have a place within the United Kingdom'. Catholic expectations were raised, dashed, and disparaged by unionist hardliners in O'Neill's party. O'Neill's paternalistic, indeed patronizing, style offended many Catholics and unionists, and his well-publicized visits to Catholic schools and meetings with the Irish Taoiseach, Séan Lemass, though unprecedented, were hardly enough in themselves to stem the tide of growing discontent. Indeed, their impact was probably greatest on the intransigent unionists who denounced O'Neill's attempts to woo recidivist Catholics. Well-meaning gestures towards Catholics could only go so far and were undermined by his need to placate unionist hardliners. This was a balancing act he was ultimately unable to sustain.

Politics in the streets

Unionist apprehension was raised by a series of protest marches organized by NICRA from 1967. The first marches were relatively peaceful, but the very fact of marching, especially through contested areas, had (and has) particularly provocative connotations in Northern Ireland and these would contribute to the rapid breakdown in law and order. The turning point is generally agreed to have been a civil rights march held in Derry in October 1968. Police turned brutally on protesters, watched by the international media and three Labour MPs. This galvanized Catholic opinion and led to the expansion of the civil rights movement among Northern Ireland's Catholic communities.

Under heavy pressure from London, O'Neill offered a five-point programme for reform later that year. It included most of the protesters' demands, but not the crucial 'one man one vote' in local government elections. To furious hardline unionists, this programme looked like capitulation to the protesters, but Catholic moderates responded cautiously though favourably and called for calm to prevent further violence. But the moderates' grip on the movement had begun to slip and the initiative was increasingly taken by more radical elements within the broader movement who had no faith in O'Neill and still less interest in a truce.

Clearly inspired by the American civil rights movement and international student politics, People's Democracy organized a 'long-march' from Belfast to Derry in January 1969. Loyalists repeatedly attacked this march, and a final, terrible confrontation occurred at Burntollet Bridge near Derry, where marchers were ambushed by a loyalist mob, including off-duty B Specials. Northern Ireland was further destabilized when a general election held the next month revealed just how split O'Neill's Ulster Unionist Party had become: ten of O'Neill's opponents from *within* his Party won seats. O'Neill resigned in April.

The end of Stormont

What was in effect a mini civil war raged in the streets of Derry and Belfast in 1969. The first policeman of what came to be known as the Troubles was killed by loyalists, and a series of UVF bombs destroyed a number of public utilities. The RUC was finding it increasingly difficult to control protests, and protests themselves were unquestionably becoming more violent and more open to involvement from both republicans and young rioters. Orange Order parades in Derry's Bogside proved to be the final straw. After the worst rioting yet and the death of five Catholics and two Protestants, the British Army was deployed to Northern Ireland in August 1969.

At the same time, the British government increased its pressure on Stormont, effectively trying to impose British standards of democracy and policing onto a deeply divided state. Virtually the whole civil rights case was vindicated by various inquiries and conceded by reforms between 1969 and 1971. Admirable though these reforms were, they stood little chance when one side saw them as too little too late, the other as a sell-out.

Loyalists had been apprehensive about increased republican agitation before the civil rights marches began. The commemoration of the Battle of the Somme and the 50th anniversary of the Easter Rising in 1966 had provoked violent clashes, and in that same year a small loyalist paramilitary group, the Ulster Volunteer Force, murdered two Catholics and one Protestant. Hints that both the Labour and Conservative parties were warming to the idea of Irish unity and the failure of the British government to recognize how reforms, especially of the police force, had alarmed loyalists, contributed to an escalation of violence.

One expression of rising Protestant apprehension was seen in the election to Westminster in 1970 of the Reverend Ian Paisley, a unionist hardliner who contributed to the collapse of traditional unionism. Paisley represented a focus for populist Protestant anger and fear. His Protestant evangelicalism, his unashamed anti-Catholicism, and his passionate outbursts at the unionists who threatened to sell Ulster down the (Liffey) river proved popular rallying cries. His important political role was confirmed by the foundation of his Democratic Unionist Party (DUP) in 1971.

Brian Faulkner succeeded James Chichester-Clark as Unionist Party leader in March 1971. A far shrewder politician than his predecessors, he included some reforming elements in his cabinet – including, remarkably, the first and last Catholic to hold office under the Stormont system – but a real conflict existed over what exactly he could do and what responsibilities the British government had assumed in the areas of policing and security.

An initially cordial relationship between Catholics and the British Army broke down quickly as Catholic areas were targeted and civilians harassed. The Social Democratic and Labour Party (SDLP), a constitutional nationalist party formed in 1970, condemned military tactics and withdrew from Stormont after the government refused to hold an inquiry into the shooting by British soldiers of two innocent Derry Catholics. This ended any productive role the SDLP might have been prepared to play in Faulkner's reforming parliament. The introduction of internment without trial probably ended any hope of wider Catholic cooperation with Stormont. A total of 342 men were picked up during the first 24 hours of the operation in August 1971. Fewer than 100 were actually IRA members, and 116 were released within 48 hours. Internment was applied exclusively to Catholics, and detainees were subjected to brutal treatment.

These arrests set off a horrific spate of violence, with 73 civilians, 11 police, and 30 soldiers being killed over the next four months. Anarchy seemed to be setting in. The denouement finally came on 'Bloody Sunday', 30 January 1972, when paratroops fired 108 rounds of ammunition on anti-internment marchers in Derry, killing 13 unarmed civilians (one more later died of gunshot wounds). None were members of the IRA. Violence escalated in the aftermath and international opinion turned against the security forces. On 24 March, Prime Minster Heath announced that Stormont would be prorogued and replaced by Direct Rule from London.

Paramilitary violence

The IRA claimed Stormont's suspension as a victory, but, though important, republican violence was only one of a number of factors that led to Stormont's failure. Nevertheless, what was unquestionably a humiliating rebuke for the unionist government provided a tremendous symbolic boost for the IRA. The IRA was strengthened by the violent events of the late 1960s, assuming the role of protector of the working class Catholic communities which bore the brunt of police and army action. This was especially important when the IRA stepped in after the over-stretched police and army did not respond to calls for help from beleaguered Catholic communities. Rough house-to-house searches, curfews, and, above all, Bloody Sunday encouraged recruitment into an organization which had been waning in preceding decades.

The IRA had split into the Provisional IRA (PIRA) and the Official IRA in 1969 over the latter's advocacy of the end of parliamentary abstention and a gradual adoption of a more socialist agenda. Sinn Féin, the political wing of the IRA, likewise split in 1970. The Officials were involved in some violent episodes in this period, but declared a permanent ceasefire in May 1972. From 1970, republican paramilitaries were responsible for the majority of killings every year, accumulating a horrific toll of over 1,800 deaths out of a total of 3,043 by 1998.

The death toll was augmented by loyalist paramilitaries. Both forming and arming civilian militias in the cause of the defence of Ulster had a long pedigree, and the events of the 1960s prompted a renewed period of such organization. In keeping with their vision of themselves as an army, the Provisionals claimed the moral high-ground because they allegedly pursued 'legitimate targets', including police and army personnel, while loyalist paramilitaries tended to engage in outright sectarian murder of Catholic civilians. Loyalists killed 700 Catholic civilians – and over 100 Protestants whom they probably mistook for Catholics – over the period of the Troubles, one of the largest categories of victim. They aimed to terrorize Catholic communities which they believed were sympathetic to the IRA and to send messages to the British and Irish governments about the consequences of British withdrawal or Irish unity.

Power sharing

Direct Rule was designed as a temporary measure. The British government believed that a return to the Stormont system was untenable and, heavily influenced by the SDLP's position, also accepted that nationalist support for devolved government was only ever likely to be achieved if an 'Irish dimension' and a role for the Irish government were part of any package. The Northern Ireland Constitution Act of 1973 formalized the government's affirmation of the principle of the reunification of the two parts of Ireland by consent only, thereby shifting the final authority on the border question from Stormont to the people of Northern Ireland. This alarmed unionists, as did the British government's acknowledgement of the right of the Irish Republic to be involved in any settlement. Both measures looked like a preface to the hated unification. A 1972 government White Paper outlined plans for a new Assembly and a power-sharing Executive.

Faulkner was in a difficult situation and his own party was split over accepting the White Paper's recommendations. Anti-White Paper unionists polled well in the first Assembly elections in 1973, leaving Faulkner's 'Official Unionists' with only a small majority of unionist support. This was to be further whittled down over the prickly Irish dimension, which was discussed at an extraordinary meeting at the civil service college at Sunningdale in December 1973. This was the first time that political leaders from the North, the South, and Britain had met for talks since 1925.

Faulkner was clearly out-manoeuvred and pressed quite hard by both nationalists and the British government into accepting the Sunningdale Agreement. This included provision for a Council of Ireland which was to enjoy 'executive and harmonizing functions'. Any reading of the agreement must see it as a major victory for the SDLP, which hoped to undermine the IRA by using the Sunningdale Agreement as proof that unity could be achieved through a constitutional and internal settlement.

In January 1974, Faulkner resigned from the leadership after losing a vote of confidence. His hope that the Sunningdale experiment would prove successful enough in operation to claw back unionist support was ruined by a British general election which allowed anti-Agreement unionists to show their strength. This they duly did, combining to form the United Ulster Unionist Council and campaigning under the slogan 'Dublin is just a Sunningdale away'. The ailing power-sharing project was finally brought down by a crippling strike organized by the Ulster Workers' Council in May 1974.

A subsequent Constitutional Convention delivered little more. Power sharing and the Irish dimension once again proved the most problematic issues. Unionists remained divided among themselves about the best way forward, with some supporting the full integration of Northern Ireland into the United Kingdom, others championing devolved government, and still others moving towards an independent Ulster policy. The Convention was wound up in 1976, depressingly little having been achieved.

The 'long war'

The IRA's strategy was chillingly simple: bomb, murder, and cause enough damage to force the British to withdraw from Northern Ireland. A ceasefire in mid-1972 and subsequent talks with the British government could be viewed as a sign of the failure of this strategy, but it could also be seen as a signal that the British government was prepared to countenance withdrawal, and thus as a kind of IRA success. The IRA's bottom line was that a cessation of violence depended entirely on a British withdrawal and that negotiations were in effect there to facilitate such an arrangement. This was not, needless to say, the view of the British government, which was eager to distance itself from Northern Ireland but was not going to be seen to be forced out by an upstart group of terrorists which deemed itself an army.

At the same time, the government sent mixed messages, hinting on more than one occasion that it would like to withdraw if 'allowed'. The truce broke down quickly and increased violence followed, culminating in Bloody Friday in July, during which 22 IRA no-warning bombs killed nine people and injured 130. 1972 proved to be the bloodiest year in all the Troubles, with 496 dead, 258 of the casualties civilian.

The 1973 Northern Ireland (Emergency Provisions) Act initiated the phasing out of political status, and foreshadowed what was to become the general 'Ulsterization' of the problem from 1975. In other words, terrorists were to be treated as normal criminals, the controversial non-jury Diplock courts were introduced, the police and the Ulster Defence Regiment were to take command of anti-IRA strategy, and internment without trial was phased out. Such strategies undoubtedly helped to stem the violence. The actual number of killings declined from the horrific peak of 1972, but the 'war' continued nonetheless, both on the British mainland and in Northern Ireland.

Another failed IRA ceasefire in 1975 triggered an acceleration in the loyalist murder campaign against Catholics, but also seemed to stimulate a shift in republican thinking. The IRA finally began to accept that a swift victory over British forces was unlikely. Neither Catholics in the North nor those in the South had sufficiently committed themselves to the IRA's aims, and the British army had not, contrary to the IRA's expectations, been forced to withdraw by unrelenting paramilitary violence. Moreover, the Irish Republic would not support the armed struggle; it was in fact convinced that any rapid British withdrawal would merely destabilize the entire island. And financial and moral support from within Northern Ireland and from important Irish-American sympathizers seemed to be shrinking.

The IRA consequently reorganized itself for a 'long war', creating cells which were independent of each other and cutting down on numbers. This helped the organization to escape infiltration and arrest and to reduce its dependence on local Catholic communities. New incentive was provided by republican prisoners in the Long Kesh internment camp (renamed the Maze Prison) who went 'on the blanket' and then staged a 'dirty protest' against the withdrawal of political status. This culminated in the 1981 hunger strikes, during which ten republican prisoners starved themselves to death: 62 people outside the Maze were killed during the hunger strike.

These acts of martyrdom struck a chord in nationalist communities but failed to move Margaret Thatcher, who refused to accede to their demands (though most were in fact later conceded). Leading hunger striker Bobby Sands won a Westminster by-election in April 1981. Over 100,000 people attended his funeral after his death the following month, reflecting significant Catholic galvanization and continuing alienation from British policy. Sands's campaign manager won the Fermanagh/South Tyrone by-election shortly afterwards. The hunger strikes hastened the republican movement's shift towards constitutional politics. At Sinn Féin's 1981 annual general meeting, director of publicity Danny Morrison famously asked 'Who here really believes we can win the war through the ballot box? But will anyone here object if, with a ballot paper in one hand and the Armalite in the other, we take power in Ireland?' The Ard Feis voted to contest local elections and, even more strikingly, to take their seats if they won. In 1986, Sinn Féin decided to take seats in the Dáil, a crucial decision which broke with the history of republican abstention and effectively recognized the partition of Ireland.

The Anglo-Irish Agreement

Sinn Féin's venture into constitutional politics, and especially its impressive showing at local and Dáil elections, motivated the SDLP and the British and Irish governments, all of whom were concerned about the possible displacement of the SDLP by Sinn Féin and the reactive side-lining of the UUP by more extreme unionists. An attempt at 'rolling devolution' in 1982 collapsed because the SDLP refused to cooperate without an Irish dimension, but cordial Anglo-Irish summits suggested that new ways forward might be found. Thatcher became convinced that the benefits of giving the Irish government an institutional role in Northern Ireland outweighed the potential risks. She sought a guarantee of Northern Ireland's constitutional position within the United Kingdom and increased cooperation between Dublin and London on security matters. After a tortuous process of negotiation, a deal, the Anglo-Irish Agreement (AIA), was finally signed in November 1985.

A permanent joint secretariat was established at Maryfield, outside Belfast, thus recognizing the Irish government's right to be consulted and heard (but not to impose policy), especially on issues concerning the Catholic minority. Importantly, the AIA explicitly guaranteed equality of treatment and recognition of the Irish and British identities of the two communities: the crucial principle of 'parity of esteem' was thus formalized. It also pledged the two governments to cross-border cooperation on a number of issues, including security. The Agreement reflected a number of ideas which had been suggested by several contemporary studies and clearly built on earlier initiatives, but it was also framed in a way that secured its own survival. It could not be destroyed by mass unionist opposition like Sunningdale had been because there was no local authority or institution to be brought down.

The Anglo-Irish Agreement was the most far-reaching and ambitious proposal produced to date by both governments. But it was also one of the most controversial and deeply unpopular among unionists, who saw it as little more than a process to facilitate a united Ireland. They were appalled by the British government's decision to force upon them an agreement which gave a voice to what they considered to be a hostile foreign government. Anti-Agreement demonstrations attracted huge crowds: about 250,000 turned out for the first one. Unionists were outraged at the lack of consultation, claiming that while the SDLP had been kept informed about the progress of talks, they had not.

Unionist MPs resigned their Westminster seats to force a poll on the issue; subsequent election results gave anti-AIA candidates a large share of the vote, but one seat was lost to the SDLP. More disturbingly, Protestant paramilitaries began to target RUC members who lived in Protestant areas for their alleged collaboration, while upping their terrorist campaign against Catholics. But unionists were divided among themselves about how to proceed on the question, and constitutional and non-parliamentary responses were framed. Opposition was virtually unanimous within the Protestant community, but it was not coherent.

Peace processes

Commentators disagree over the success or otherwise of the AIA. A 1989 review pronounced it disappointing in terms of improvement in security or inter-community relations. The SDLP gained the most from the Agreement, but seemed intent on using it to promote a form of joint authority rather than power sharing, an option which heightened unionist suspicions. Sinn Féin's electoral popularity had been stemmed, but it had probably peaked before the signing of the AIA in any case. In the meantime, the IRA's violent campaign continued: an appalling 1987 bombing of a Remembrance Day service at Enniskillen killed 11 Protestant civilians, but cost the IRA dearly in propaganda terms. A number of key figures began to suspect that the IRA might be ready to move towards conventional politics, or at least might be willing to discuss such a step.

Controversial talks between SDLP leader John Hume and Sinn Féin president Gerry Adams in 1988 produced no tangible results, but the scene was set for further discussions. As always, each party had to convince its constituents that its fundamental objectives were not compromised by these talks. This delicate strategy was to underpin all the negotiations which led to the historic Good Friday Agreement of 1998. This in effect meant that unionists had to be convinced that they were not being corralled into a united Ireland, while republicans had to be able to claim that any agreement allowed progress towards unity. This was and remains the most difficult problem: how to conciliate both nationalists and unionists without provoking the breakdown of constitutional politics, a violent backlash, or both.

The Good Friday Agreement

A complex and often fraught series of negotiations led up to what the IRA described as a 'total cessation of operations' in 1994, not the permanent abandonment of violence which Unionists and the British government sought, but a significant achievement in itself, especially given that the British government had not promised any concrete concessions in return. Loyalist paramilitaries followed suit shortly afterwards, announcing their own ceasefire. The lead-up to the ceasefires had actually seen an acceleration of violence, and the ceasefire itself did not end the gangsterism which thrived among paramilitaries: punishment beatings and harassment remained a fact of Northern Irish life.

The main stumbling block became decommissioning: unionists and the British government insisted that the IRA must begin this process before any all-party talks could begin. This demand was highly unlikely to be met, and there was no international precedent for such an insistence. The Mitchell Commission of 1996 recommended that talks could be held in tandem and not strictly after decommissioning, but this was rejected by the Major government. An enormous IRA bomb in London's Canary Wharf in 1996 – which killed two and injured over 100 – ended the ceasefire, but a new truce the following year allowed the admission of Sinn Féin into all-party talks.

Real impetus was given by the involvement in the process of Bill

16. A loyalist mural from Mount Vernon Road in Belfast, depicting the emblems of the UVF, the Protestant Action Force, and the Young Citizen Volunteers. Painted in 1995, it reflects the loyalist paramilitaries' willingness to participate in a ceasefire, but also their readiness to recommence hostilities if necessary.

Clinton and Senator George Mitchell, who helped to propel all parties towards the negotiating table. Moreover, Tony Blair, who was elected with a massive majority in 1997, espoused soft unionist sympathies, while also displaying a real determination and flexibility to keep the peace process moving. The Good Friday Agreement, signed in April 1998, depended on compromise and pragmatism from all parties. Few people who watched anxiously as the talks threatened to break down until the very end will ever forget the moment when the deal was finally sealed. Though the Agreement was built on precedents, it nevertheless required both republicans and unionists to give way much more than they ever had before, and indeed a good deal more than many commentators had predicted.

A referendum on the Agreement revealed overwhelming Catholic support, while unionists were split almost down the middle. Polls suggest that just over half of Northern Ireland's Protestants voted for the Agreement. There is no doubt that Catholics and Protestants voted for different interpretations of the Agreement. The marketability of the Agreement depended on its ability to appeal to the majority of both communities. Both Gerry Adams and Unionist Party leader David Trimble expended a great deal of interpretative and linguistic ingenuity in selling the Agreement as a safeguard of the Union on the one hand and a stepping-stone to Irish unity on the other.

Both experienced significant opposition: the Ulster Unionist Council stood by Trimble, but the DUP, the Orange Order, and six of the UUP's ten MPs opposed it. Crucially, however, both the main loyalist paramilitary groups and their political wings gave support. The 'Real IRA' had already been formed by a splinter group which opposed Sinn Féin's move towards participation in government. In 1998 it planted a bomb at Omagh which killed 29 people, the worst single atrocity of the Troubles. Censured by hostile public opinion, the Real IRA called a ceasefire and only the obscure Continuity IRA remained 'at war'.

17. A republican mural which parodies the 'Keep Britain Tidy' anti-litter campaign in Dromintee, South Armagh, 2000. The Good Friday Agreement has not put a halt to such sentiment.

What did the Agreement achieve? It established a 108-member assembly which would be elected by proportional representation. It was power sharing with a twist: majority domination was checked by a series of measures including special voting procedures. Parity of esteem was re-emphasized, and promises were made about reforms in policing, security, and justice. In addition, a North-South Ministerial Council was established. Republicans finally dropped their abstentionist stand and took up seats in the new assembly. This was a recognition of the legal existence of Northern Ireland, the consent principle, and the primacy of constitutional politics. Thus, Trimble could argue that the Agreement strengthened unionism: it replaced the hated Anglo-Irish Agreement, provided the devolved government with a power of veto over the North-South bodies and a British-Irish Council.

Delays in decommissioning and arguments about police reform dogged the peace process. Nevertheless, both Trimble and Adams just about managed to maintain enough of a hold over their constituents to heave the process forward. Each of the Agreement's architects in London, Dublin, and Belfast has displayed a steely determination to make it work, marginalizing opponents and arguably overlooking constitutional norms in the process. Such strategies have not, however, managed to stem the growing tide of opposition to the Agreement within a disillusioned Protestant community.

Writing about a process which is changing on an almost daily basis rules out conclusion, but it does invite speculation. This most delicate of agreements held up much longer than many predicted, and it allowed for the extraordinary spectacle of former gunmen participating in the governance of a province which until recently they refused to recognize, let alone administer. Equally remarkably, unionists sat on committees and even in the Executive alongside the hardened republicans with whom they refused to negotiate for decades. Turbulent, potholed, and jagged though this recent attempt to find peace may be, it is by far the most promising to date, and is even being viewed as a model for peace processes around the world.

Power sharing and parity of esteem must form the core of any lasting settlement in Northern Ireland; even the most stubborn enemies of the current process have acknowledged that. Perhaps the greatest obstacle to peace remains the entrenched sectarian and polarized attitudes which no peace process can dissolve. The reflexive recourse to communal violence remains as potent as ever, reminding us that ancient suspicions linger while national identities remain contested.

Chapter 8
Modern Ireland

Ireland in the 1950s experienced 'a dark night of the soul in which doubts were prevalent as to whether the achievement of political independence had not been futile'. This gloomy judgement by a perceptive observer was borne out in the immediate post-war years when Ireland failed to live up to the ambitions of its hopeful founders: partition was entrenched, emigration soared, and the economy went into seemingly terminal decline.

Yet, in the final third of the 20th century, the Republic of Ireland underwent significant, sometimes spectacular, social and economic change. Ireland's politicians and civil servants expressed a growing willingness to look abroad for investment and ideas, gradually freeing the country from its self-imposed autarkic straightjacket. From the 1950s, such bread and butter issues as wages, standards of living, and social reform began to outflank the 'national question' and the old civil war divide as electoral priorities, while some older assumptions about authentic Irish identity and Ireland's place in the world underwent far-reaching revision.

Political shifts

The Irish electorate expressed its dissatisfaction with the *status quo* at the general election of 1948 which was fought against a background of industrial action, shortages, and sleaze allegations: the latter was to re-emerge as one of the discreditable constants of Irish political life. The establishment of several new political parties and the revival of the Labour Party also helped to nudge Fianna Fáil out of office for the first time since 1932. The most important of these was Clann na Poblachta, founded in 1946. It had little in common with the uninspiring Fine Gael, Labour, or Clann na Talmhan (a farmers' party), apart from a desire to remove from power the apparently perennial de Valera. This was enough to compel these seemingly incompatible parties into the first inter-party government in 1948. The era of coalition government had begun.

Fine Gael's John A. Costello, a compromise candidate, became Taoiseach. His greatest moment came in 1948 when he declared at an Ottawa press conference that Ireland would become a republic. His colleagues were stunned by this declaration, and quite why he took the unexpected decision at that time remains a matter of debate. The advent of the Republic of Ireland failed to excite the Irish population, likely because it merely legalized a political status which had in reality prevailed since 1937.

Though at variance in some ways, the inter-party government could nonetheless communally promote its piety, famously telegraphing the Pope after its first cabinet meeting to assure him of its resolve 'to strive for the attainment of social order in Ireland based on Christian principles'. These lofty aspirations were, however, called into question during what became known as the 'mother and child scheme'. Spearheaded by the reforming minister Dr Noel Browne, it aimed to provide free healthcare for mothers and for children under the age of 16. This voluntary proposal provoked an outcry among the hierarchy and the medical profession, who warned of the dangers to the family of 'socialized medicine'. This led to a very public political crisis during which the church, the medical profession, and, ultimately, the government itself, snubbed Browne, who was finally ditched by his own party.

Browne's exit failed to save the coalition. Weak and in a minority, Fianna Fáil nevertheless limped back to power under de Valera after the 1951 election. This lasted only until 1954 when a second inter-party government was formed, only to be replaced yet again by a large Fianna Fáil majority in 1957. Fianna Fáil remained in power until 1973, though de Valera finally stood down as Taoiseach in 1959 and was replaced by his appointed successor, Sean Lemass. The indomitable Dev refused to fade gracefully into old age, becoming president in 1959 and remaining in that office until his eventual retirement in 1973.

Between 1973 and 1998, there were 12 changes of government and a proliferation of coalition governments. Economic difficulties shook fragile alliances and proved to be the undoing of most of these short-lived governments, though political corruption in the later years also undermined a disconcerting number of them. Passports, beef, guns, and department stores became matters for speculation and investigation as one scandal after another was revealed to an appalled public. The 1980s did, however, see the premierships of two of Ireland's most redoubtable politicians and the development of a vigorous political competition between the two main parties not seen since the early days of the state. The contrast between Fianna Fáil's Charles Haughey and Garret Fitzgerald of Fine Gael was conspicuous: the former a charismatic but tainted survivor of scandal and sleaze allegations, the latter a modernizing intellectual. Both men nonetheless added a much-needed spark to the atrophying world of parliamentary politics.

Fianna Fáil was forced into its first coalition government in 1989, signifying the end of its halcyon days of solitary political hegemony. Alliances became more vibrant with the revival of the Labour Party and the establishment of the Progressive Democrats in 1985, an offshoot from the liberal wing of Fianna Fáil. Both parties served in coalitions, Labour combining with Fianna Fáil in 1993, and then with Fine Gael and the Democratic Left in 1994. This government was replaced by another Fianna Fáil–Progressive Democrat alliance under the leadership of Bertie Ahern in 1997.

Economic planning

Irish governments faced severe social and economic challenges in the post-war years. Yet, commitment to the essential changes which were needed to turn the country around were delivered sporadically, while politicians continued to live in stubborn denial about the flaws that lay at the heart of the country's economic and social structures. The most pressing concerns were poor economic performance and the continuing exodus of large numbers of people. By 1961, the population had fallen to 2.8 million, an all-time low. Between 1951 and 1956, almost 200,000 people emigrated, and another 210,000 followed in the second half of the decade. A staggering four out of every five children born in the 1930s left Ireland in the 1950s. Why?

The fundamental problem was the same one that had encouraged millions to emigrate in the 19th century: a dearth of opportunity and work. Between 1946 and 1961, the number of people working in agriculture declined by one-third and the number of small farms declined still further. The only agricultural product to prosper was cattle, precisely the sector the government had hoped to reduce. At the same time, the more labour-intensive market in pigs, eggs, and tillage contracted.

The 1950s are described by most commentators as dreary, mediocre, and disappointing. Europe was generally demoralized in the post-war years, but most of Western Europe at least enjoyed an economic boom between 1949 and 1956, while Ireland witnessed a doubling of its balance of payments deficit, the growth of unemployment, and a relative decline in living standards. The war years had, however, allowed a greater centralization of government and increased emphasis on economic planning. Fianna Fáil's 1945 welfarist Public Health Bill, the establishment of the Irish

Development Authority in 1949, and the drawing up of plans to accompany applications for Marshall Aid suggested that Ireland was prepared to adopt a more modern and internationally attuned economy. Accordingly, the existing acceptance of state centralization and Keynesian economic policy was accelerated from the late 1950s.

Civil servants, particularly T. K. Whitaker, Secretary of the Department of Finance, directed much of the drive towards progressive economic planning under the broadly supportive aegis of Lemass. Whitaker's celebrated *Economic Development* White Paper of 1958 formed the basis for the first Programme for Economic Expansion. Two further programmes followed in 1963–8 and 1969–72. The main recommendations included five-year economic plans, a move away from protectionism, and increased orientation of agricultural goods for foreign markets. Unexciting though they may seem to modern readers, these plans in fact repudiated many of the economic shibboleths that had underpinned economic policy since the foundation of the state, and represented a genuinely new and dynamic dispensation which encouraged foreign investment.

Though not exceptional by international standards, the Irish economy did display real signs of improvement quite rapidly. National income rose by an unprecedented annual average of 3%, and over 350 foreign companies set up bases in Ireland during the 1960s. The result was not an unmitigated success, and economic improvement was encouraged by a range of factors in addition to planning. The crucial shift was, however, greater Irish involvement in the world economy.

Encouragingly, too, emigration began to decline and the population increased for the first time since the Famine, reaching 3.2 million by the 1980s. Further important advances were made in areas such as tourism. From 1955, Bord Failte Éireann presided over an expanding tourist market, accelerated massively by transatlantic flights and improved infrastructure from the 1960s. By the early 1990s, over 3 million people were visiting Ireland annually and about 7% of Ireland's GDP derived from tourism. But becoming further integrated in international markets had its pitfalls as well as its rewards. Ireland's economy was rocked, for example, by the oil crises of the 1970s, which disrupted an already vulnerable economy.

Nor could it protect it from mismanagement at the hands of both major parties. During the 1970s, economic growth simply could not keep up with demand, and Fianna Fáil's promises of bread and circuses during the 1977 election campaign did not reflect the reality of the massive increase in government spending and borrowing. The three general elections in 18 months between 1981 and 1982 were largely fought on economic issues as no party seemed to be able to manage the ailing economy. Unemployment climbed once again, and emigration became an attractive option for more and more people. A 1984 'Building on Reality' programme failed to stop the rot, and the national debt reached a staggering IR£24 billion by 1987, while unemployment soared to a woeful 18%.

Having condemned severe economic cuts during the 1987 election campaign, Fianna Fáil itself initiated stringent budgetary reform after forming a coalition government with the Progressive Democrats. Strikingly, too, Fine Gael asserted support for its rival's attempts to stabilize the economy: this did nothing for its own electoral standing, but it did highlight the seriousness of the problem. A period of severe cost-cutting followed, producing a number of the desired results. Two crucial deals were struck between the government and its 'social partners' (mainly farmers, trade unions, and employers): the Programme for Economic and Social Progress and the Programme for National Recovery. How much these contributed to economic improvement remains debatable, but the crippling issue of public sector pay had had to be addressed.

Significant improvement was recorded in the early 1990s, but a currency crisis and spiralling unemployment in 1992 confirmed that economic stability was by no means secure. Yet, a remarkable growth rate of 7% was maintained after 1993, living standards shot up, and the national debt declined. By the mid-1990s, economic growth in Ireland was – extraordinarily – higher than anywhere else in the Western world.

The Irish economy is certainly more diverse and sophisticated than hitherto, and this has helped to integrate it more fully into the global economy. By the 1990s, Ireland's was a modern industrial economy producing sophisticated goods, but reliance on the agricultural sector remained high. The 'Celtic Tiger' went from strength to strength, but welfare provision did not keep up with the rising costs of living, especially in Dublin. The days of economic stagnation had gone, but designer stores and plush restaurants cannot conceal persistent social problems, including poverty, drug abuse, exceptionally high rates of teenage pregnancy, and the appalling treatment of some refugees.

Ireland and Europe

Ireland's admission to the United Nations in 1955 was a significant step forward in the process of international assimilation, but much the most important was membership of the EEC from 1973, ratified by a large majority in a 1972 referendum. The practical impact of EEC membership is clear: between 1973 and 1991, Ireland received IR£14 billion from the European Community. In 1991 Ireland contributed IR£348.3 million to the EEC, while receiving IR£2.2 billion. In other words, Ireland got back six pounds for every one it sent to the Community. The European golden goose could not guard Ireland from international slumps, but her eggs were reliable and regular. They also made a demonstrable difference to the economy in important ways. The Common Agricultural Policy boosted the income of farmers, for example, and European membership helped to stimulate foreign investment.

The overall impact of these developments remains questionable. One could argue, for example, that rich agricultural subsidies merely threw a life rope to a deteriorating sector. The establishment of foreign companies has also provided mixed blessings: more jobs, but a greater share of profits going abroad. But membership has generated a fundamental psychological shift, as Ireland has been able to distance itself from Britain's economic and political orbit. This was best demonstrated by Ireland's decision to join the European Monetary System in 1979, breaking its historic connection with sterling. The country's adoption in 1998 of the single European currency, the euro, underlined this repositioning, especially as Britain opted out.

Political and economic relations between the two countries have been largely cordial and often mutually beneficial, demonstrating the weakening of older suspicions and animosities. Significantly, too, Ireland's economic relationship with the Continent grew as its dependence on British markets declined. By 1996, 26% of Irish exports went to Britain, while 48% went to Continental Europe; a huge shift from 56% to the UK and 17.6% to the Continent in 1973.

Dublin – Belfast – London

An increasingly close Anglo-Irish relationship has had a largely beneficial and innovative impact on the Northern Ireland question. Both countries have eased their hardline positions on the question of Northern Ireland's sovereignty, though Britain has moved more radically on this question by accepting the idea of unification by consent without strings, while Ireland has similarly accepted the consent principle, but continues to aspire to Irish unity, in however diluted a form.

Ireland has had two major aims since the 1960s: to serve as guardian of northern Catholics and to ensure that its own economic and social stability is not endangered by events in Northern Ireland. Some horrendous acts of violence have spilled over the border, but the Republic has largely succeeded in both these aims, through its stringent internal legislation and its support for non-violent nationalism. Its advocacy of the constitutional SDLP and insistence on an 'Irish dimension' in any settlement were reflected most clearly in The New Ireland Forum which discussed these issues between 1983 and 1984. Strongly supported by Garret Fitzgerald and John Hume, it included all the major constitutional nationalist parties, North and South, in the creation of a blueprint for negotiations with the British government. It expressed the customary aspiration to unity, but more creatively flagged the possibilities of joint British-Irish authority and a federal state.

Though unacceptable to Thatcher and anathema to unionists, the Forum Report unquestionably contributed to the evolution of the Anglo-Irish Agreement. This Agreement marked a significant step forward in Anglo-Irish relations and the institutionalization of many of the core principles which were subsequently enshrined in the Good Friday Agreement. The Anglo-Irish Agreement also set the tenor of subsequent settlements and declarations by confirming the strategy of joint government action and pronunciation on Northern Irish initiatives.

The generally cordial relationship between Dublin and London made it increasingly difficult for Sinn Féin to maintain its opposition to involvement in 'peace talks'. Neither Sinn Féin nor the IRA could any longer afford to delude itself about the friendliness of Dublin governments. Certainly, Dublin looked more willing at first than its London counterpart to be flexible about accommodating the men and women of violence, but that accommodation was premised on an end to hostilities and the necessity for republicans to earn an electoral mandate. Such a strategy was, however, abhorrent to many unionists and British politicians who equated 'wooing terrorists' with capitulation to violence.

Yet, this was in essence the strategy pursued by both governments in the 1990s, supported by the American government, which famously granted Gerry Adams a 48-hour US visa in 1994. The challenge was to give Sinn Féin sufficient political dividends to ensure its continuing involvement in negotiations, while at the same time inducing it to concede enough to keep unionists on board. This was a task whose difficulty cannot be underestimated and whose success rested on a combination of coercion, flattery, compromise, and fudge. The signing of the Good Friday Agreement in 1998 was a tribute to enormously improved Anglo-Irish relations, but, above all, it was a testament to the pragmatism that had come to characterize both governments' Northern Irish policy.

The Republic has clearly replaced simplistic older assumptions about national unity with a more sophisticated position which takes unionist opinion and identity more seriously into account. But some old attitudes linger. The Irish public voted overwhelmingly to remove articles two and three from the Irish constitution, but they were replaced by new wordings which, while they embrace diversity, also back eventual Irish unity. The rhetoric of unification is cheap and evocative, but the Republic is no West Germany. Romantic notions about the 'fourth green field' cannot disguise the fact that the Republic is neither willing nor able to take on Northern Ireland's economic problems as well as a million resentful Protestants, even if the opportunity existed. The island of Ireland in reality consists of two Irelands. Peaceful co-existence with the North, some involvement in its affairs, and maximum reliance on the British exchequer's subsidization of the province suits the Republic much more than it is ready to admit.

Public and private morality

In 1979 over one-third of Ireland's population turned out to greet Pope John Paul II at Dublin's Phoenix Park. This remarkable demonstration of popular piety was confirmed by surveys which suggested that over 90% of the population went to Mass at least once a week in the 1970s. This was the highest rate in Western Europe; interestingly, Northern Ireland boasted the second highest.

Yet, both observance and compliance with Church teaching have changed rapidly in the last four decades. Mass attendance has fallen, dramatically in some working-class areas, and surveys confirm that levels of belief and observance continue to decline, particularly among young people.

Legislative safeguarding of Catholic social teaching has been tested amidst a good deal of debate and acrimony. Private behaviour has, however, been clearly well in advance of public pronouncements on contraception, homosexuality, and abortion. The 1968 Papal encyclical, *Humanae Vitae*, banned artificial contraception, but it is estimated, for example, that over 40,000 Irish women used the contraceptive pill by 1974, and that from 1980 about 10 million condoms were sold annually in the Irish Republic.

In 1974 the Supreme Court upheld the right of a 27-year-old mother of four to import contraceptive jelly for her own use, triggering a new campaign for the liberalization of legislation. After much lobbying, the Health (Family Planning) Bill was finally published in late 1978 and was appositely described by the then Minister for Health, Charles Haughey, as 'an Irish bill for an Irish problem'. This complex bill in effect allowed contraception by prescription, the unwritten assumption being to married couples only. In defiance of opposition from Fianna Fáil and the Catholic hierarchy, a 1985 bill made contraceptives available to anyone over 18.

The remaining problem was the sale of contraceptives from vending machines. Many doctors and health workers supported such sales, especially in the context of the growing AIDS problem and the restricted opening hours of many health centres and chemists where condoms could be purchased. Though the authorities usually ignored illegal vending machines which had been set up in college and university bars, for example, the issue was finally brought to a head in 1990 when the Irish Family Planning Association was fined for selling condoms in Dublin's

Virgin Megastore. The £500 fine was paid on behalf of the Family Planning Association by the rock band U2, and an embarrassed government began a legislative process that led eventually to a 1993 bill which removed all remaining restrictions on the sale and supply of condoms.

Debates about abortion proved to be far more controversial and legally complex, as the 'pro-life' lobby mounted a fierce campaign to have abortion explicitly proscribed in the 1937 constitution. A confusing amendment whose precise meaning was uncertain was passed by referendum in 1983, though about 4,000 women continued to travel to Britain annually to obtain abortions in the 1980s. The tragic case of a 14-year-old girl who had been raped but was prevented by the High Court from leaving Ireland for a termination in 1992 induced a painful national debate on the issue of women's access to travel and information about abortion. The Supreme Court overturned the High Court's decision under great public pressure, allowing the girl to leave Ireland, but insisted that this was only permitted in cases where the mother's life was in grave danger.

This left the 1983 amendment in doubt and forced a further referendum on the issue. The results were mixed and in essence the vote revealed that Irish people affirmed a woman's right to information about abortion and to travel abroad to get one, but not to have one in her own country. This equivocation has yet to be resolved, but probably reflects quite accurately the ambiguous nature of public opinion on the issue.

The Irish parliament passed legislation in 1993 which decriminalized homosexual acts between consenting adults over the age of 17 amid little controversy. Divorce, however, proved to be more contentious, especially as it was proscribed under the constitution. A 1986 referendum which aimed to lift the ban was defeated decisively, despite the fact that many thousands of people were believed to be caught in broken marriages or unofficially

separated. A further referendum held in 1995 repealed the
constitutional ban, but only by a tiny margin.

This vote revealed once again how tentatively the Irish public was
willing to judge on the moral questions which a modernizing society
was compelled to address, especially in the context of membership
of the EEC. Irish citizens could and did appeal to the European
courts in matters of private moral choice, and the ratification of the
Maastricht Treaty in particular opened new cans of worms about
the compatibility of Irish legislation (notably on abortion) with
Europe's. Yet, the fact that the divorce referendum was passed the
second time around also reveals that attitudes were changing, and
changing quite quickly. The first divorce in independent Ireland
was awarded in January 1997.

The Catholic Church

The days when Irish bishops saw it as both their duty and their right
to advise the Irish public on how to exercise their political mandate
have long gone. No public guidance was given on the Maastricht
Treaty referendum in 1992, a real departure from customary
practice. One explanation for this is the seeming detachment of the
Church from ordinary life. A crisis has, for example, developed in
the area of vocations: young people are simply not taking orders in
sufficient numbers to maintain the kind of physical presence the
Church had come to enjoy over the last two centuries. The number
of religious personnel declined from 25,172 in 1970 to 15,643 in
1989. Only 3.6% of religious workers in 1989 were under 30 years
old, and the average age continues to rise.

The Church's moral authority has also been called into question by
a number of scandals which have eroded public confidence. One of
the most notorious was the case of Éamonn Casey, the popular
Bishop of Galway. The bishop resigned in mysterious circumstances
in 1992, and revelations about his affair with an American woman
and the child he fathered in 1973 hit the headlines soon afterwards.

Further revelations about paedophile priests and the abuse by some Christian Brothers of boys in their care added to the sense of disillusionment. But what was perhaps most revealing about these squalid disclosures was the frank character of their discussion in the media. Public criticism of clerics was virtually unthinkable in previous decades, as was the now open discussion about such sensitive issues as clerical celibacy. The loosening of the deference once shown to the Church is perhaps the most obvious manifestation of the reality of the secularization of Irish society.

The position of women

Equality between men and women has not been achieved in Ireland, just as it has not been achieved in comparable Western societies. But the sheer prevalence of discussion about this issue suggests that women's roles are now a taken-for-granted measure of tolerance and progress. The most outstanding symbol of the recent shift in public perceptions of the status of women in Irish society was the election in 1990 of Mary Robinson to the Irish presidency. Not only was she Ireland's first female president, she was also a distinguished lawyer and a seasoned campaigner for the liberalization of divorce and contraception law.

Mary Robinson is hardly representative of most Irish women, who are well represented in the membership of all the major political parties (about 40%), but under-represented in national executives and in the Dáil. Women of her seniority and prominence remain rare. One of the most remarkable aspects of the Robinson phenomenon is in fact the level of popularity and affection such a seemingly atypical woman won from the Irish public. She coincided with a period of brisk social change and was an ideal representative of the new modern and progressive Ireland – an image the country was eager to present to the world. But she was also a product of the steady and often unglamorous campaign sustained for decades by the Irish women's movement.

Like many comparable movements, the Irish feminist movement enjoyed its glory days in the early 20th century before retreating during the inhibited and conservative mid-century. In the last decades of the 20th century, it returned with a bang, most famously in 1971 when 47 members of Irish Women's Liberation took a 'contraception train' from Belfast to Dublin, flagrantly importing contraceptives from Northern Ireland in the face of embarrassed officials. These women forced onto a largely unwilling and disapproving Irish public a frank discussion about women's sexual and political rights. Issues like abortion and birth control were the focus of women's campaigns throughout the Western world, but the Irish campaign was exceptionally hindered by the overwhelmingly Catholic ethos of the country. Unsurprisingly, Ireland trailed behind Britain and the United States, each of which reformed laws governing contraception before the Irish government could be persuaded to do so, but it also fell behind France, Spain, and Italy.

Both the work of activists and European directives has allowed Irish women an unprecedented measure of legal protection in the workforce and in their private lives. This has not, however, resulted in vast improvements in employment opportunities. An Anti-Discrimination (Pay) Act was introduced in 1974, but in 1992 Irish women received less than 70% of male earnings. There was a sharp increase of 54.6% in the female labour force between 1971 and 1992. But this seemingly impressive figure is partly a consequence of the growing demand for low-paid and part-time workers in the service industry.

Statistics can, of course, be used to make all sorts of cases, but the reality in Ireland is that despite some qualifications, women's roles are changing and changing rapidly. The Celtic Tiger relies on women's labour, and more and more families rely on two wages. Female participation and performance statistics in secondary education are now equal to or better than male rates, and women make up just over half of all undergraduate and postgraduate students in Irish universities. Educated women are no longer compelled to leave professional employment on marriage: there was in fact a seven-fold increase in the number of married women in the Irish workforce between 1951 and 1991, along with a significant shift from agriculture to the industry, service, and professional sectors. By 1996, more married than single women were engaged in paid employment. The constitutional affirmation of 'women's life within the home' looked increasingly pointless.

Irish married women are less likely to work outside the home than most of their European counterparts, but a steady trend has begun and there is no sign of its slowing down. This has become possible because of the decline in the fertility rate. In 1951 this stood at 6.0 children per woman of childbearing age. By 1994, this had dropped to 1.85, indicating a secularizing society and proactive attitudes towards family planning. Irish women still have more children than their European counterparts, though marriage and cohabitation patterns largely conform to European norms. What this seems to suggest, yet again, is that personal decisions often do not correlate with public religious observance.

Modern Ireland

How modern is modern Ireland? Traditionalists will point out that Ireland retains many of the characteristics which have underpinned its national culture for decades: Mass attendance remains the highest in Western Europe; holy relics and shrines dot the landscape and can even be found in central Dublin's O'Connell Street, where taxis park under the watchful eye of a blue Madonna. Could she talk, however, she would no doubt speak of the momentous changes she has witnessed during her residency, of the contrast between the crowds who lined up to greet the Pope and the crowds who marched, only a few years later, to protest against Ireland's antiquated laws on contraception, divorce, and abortion.

Madonnas do of course talk in Ireland; they also move, bleed, and smile, at shrines in Knock and a number of other mainly rural locations. Pilgrimage enjoyed a resurgence in the 1980s and continues to draw crowds who pray at holy sites around the country, many no doubt for the salvation of the new and immoral Ireland. Such observance has probably been strengthened in reaction to the secularization of the State, but it is difficult not to conclude that it is fighting a losing battle. A serious pious devotion to Catholicism remains, but this is a flexible devotion which is increasingly learning to live alongside an individualist approach to modern life in which personal choice is paramount. In this way, Irish Catholics are becoming more like the millions of their fellow Catholics in the Western world, who similarly subscribe to the rituals of the Church, while ignoring its moral teaching in their personal lives. Reticence about abortion reform is neither uncommon nor particularly Irish. It is an issue which divides societies around the world, Catholic and non-Catholic. Ambiguity about this issue cannot be seen merely as proof of tenacious Catholicism.

Modernization is not an insular business: it occurs in a broader context and develops through exposure to outside ideas and trends. Ireland is in many ways as modern as comparable Western countries. It has experienced a frantic period of 'catch-up', but is now fully integrated into the global economy and is thus compelled to balance 'national identity' with the homogenizing demands of global corporatism. As in Paris, Sydney, and Beijing, it aims to preserve distinctiveness while accommodating the ubiquitous McDonalds and Starbucks. But quite what distinctiveness amounts to is difficult to quantify, as it is for any national community.

Many older, sometimes imagined, distinctly Irish features have faded. Certainly, the Irish language has continued to decline. The compulsory Irish language requirement for a pass in the Intermediate and Leaving Certificates was abolished in 1973–4, as was Irish for most civil service positions. A significant and very modern step was taken in 1996 when the Irish-language television station, Telefís na Gaeilge, began transmission. Nevertheless, many predict the extinction of the Gaeltacht (the Irish-speaking areas of the country). A 1983 Bord na Gaeilge study concluded that only 4% of the population spoke Irish on a daily basis. But, like religion, an accommodation has been reached with the country's Gaelic past: Irish names remain popular, Celtic imagery is prolific, and traditional music retains a loyal following.

At the same time, Irish literary culture in English – especially poetry and drama – maintains its traditionally high international profile. The prodigiously talented W. B. Yeats, James Joyce, and their contemporaries have been followed by a long line of gifted Irish writers, including Samuel Beckett and Seamus Heaney, both, like Yeats, Nobel Prize winners. The export of popular culture, through film and music in particular, also remains vibrant and lucrative. The high-profile involvement in human rights and liberal causes of such artists as U2's Bono, Bob Geldof, and Sinead O'Connor has likewise contributed to the transformation of Ireland's image across the world.

A sometimes cynical and certainly financially savvy approach to 'Irishness' has also become pronounced. The country markets itself cleverly and self-consciously to tourists who wish to experience 'authentic Ireland', while at the same time catering to golfers, fishers, stag dos, and sports enthusiasts. This is no different from successful tourist operations around the globe. Such marketing has spread beyond Ireland's shores through the remarkable phenomenon of 'Irish pubs'. Almost every major city around the world now boasts a bar festooned with Guinness paraphernalia and signs announcing the distance to Cork, Galway, and Dublin.

Contemporary Ireland is a modern and dynamic country whose booming economy remains a source of envy and wonder. The pace of change continues to astound visitors, especially those who knew Ireland before the Celtic Tiger began to roar. Unashamed expressions of once unthinkable heterodoxy in religious, sexual, and artistic matters are good indicators of the gradual but palpable decay of the social conservatism that once saturated the country.

The first two decades of the 20th century brought Ireland independence, but the final two brought a social revolution whose consequences were probably even more far-reaching. They have shaped profoundly the contours of modern Irish life.

Further reading

A great many excellent monographs and articles cover the issues raised in this book. For reasons of brevity I have included only a small selection, but each listed text contains invaluable advice on further reading.

General surveys

J. Bardon, *A History of Ulster* (Blackstaff, 1992).

D. G. Boyce, *Nationalism in Ireland* (Routledge, 1982, 1991, 1995).

T. Brown, *Ireland: A Social and Cultural History, 1922-85* (Fontana, 1985).

L. M. Cullen, *The Emergence of Modern Ireland, 1600-1900* (Batsford, 1981).

M. E. Daly, *Social and Economic History of Ireland since 1800* (Dublin Educational Co., 1981).

D. Fitzpatrick, *The Two Irelands, 1912-1939* (Oxford University Press, 1998).

R. F. Foster, *Modern Ireland, 1600-1972* (Allen Lane, 1988).

K. T. Hoppen, *Ireland since 1800: Conflict and Conformity* (Longman, 1989, 1999).

A. Jackson, *Ireland, 1878-1998* (Blackwell, 1999).

J. J. Lee, *Ireland, 1912-85* (Cambridge University Press, 1989).

F. S. L. Lyons, *Ireland Since the Famine* (Fontana, 1971, 1973).

C. O'Grada, *Ireland: A New Economic History, 1780-1939* (Clarendon Press, 1994).

C. Townshend, *Ireland: The Twentieth Century* (Arnold, 1999).

Late 18th- and early 19th-century Ireland

T. Bartlett, *The Fall and Rise of the Irish Nation: The Catholic Question, 1690–1830* (Gill and Macmillan, 1992).

S. Connolly, *Religion and Society in Nineteenth-Century Ireland* (Economic and Social History Society of Ireland, 1985, 1987, 1994).

M. E. Daly, *The Famine in Ireland* (Dublin Historical Association, 1986).

D. Fitzpatrick, *Irish Emigration, 1801–1921* (Economic and Social History Society of Ireland, 1984).

C. O'Grada, *Black '47 and Beyond: The Great Irish Famine in History, Economy and Memory* (Princeton University Press, 1999).

G. Ó'Tuathaigh, *Ireland Before the Famine* (Gill and Macmillan, 1991).

The land question

P. Bew, *Land and the National Question in Ireland, 1858–1882* (Gill and Macmillan, 1978).

P. Bull, *Land, Politics and Nationalism: A Study of the Irish Land Question* (Gill and Macmillan, 1996).

W. E. Vaughan, *Landlords and Tenants in Ireland, 1884–1904* (Economic and Social History Society of Ireland, 1984).

The national question

P. Bew, *Conflict and Conciliation in Ireland, 1880–1910: Parnellites and Radical Agrarians* (Clarendon Press, 1987).

R. V. Comerford, *The Fenians in Context: Irish Politics and Society, 1848–1882* (Wolfhound Press, 1982, 1998).

John Kendle, *Ireland and the Federal Solution: The Debate over the United Kingdom Constitution, 1870–1921* (McGill-Queens University Press, 1989).

L. O'Broin, *Revolutionary Underground: The Story of the Irish Republican Brotherhood, 1858–1924* (Gill and Macmillan, 1976).

Ulster Unionism

P. Bew, *Ideology and the Irish Question: Ulster Unionism and Ulster Nationalism* (Clarendon Press, 1994).

P. Buckland, *Ulster Unionism and the Origins of Northern Ireland, 1886–1922* (Gill and Macmillan, 1973).

Alvin Jackson, *The Ulster Party: Irish Unionists in the House of Commons, 1884–1911* (Clarendon Press, 1989).

J. Loughlin, *Gladstone, Home Rule and the Ulster Question, 1882–1893* (Gill and Macmillan, 1986).

Early 20th-century Ireland

D. Fitzpatrick, *Politics and Irish Life: Provincial Experiences of War and Revolution, 1913–1923* (Gill and Macmillan, 1977; Cork University Press, 1998).

A. Gailey, *Ireland and the Death of Kindness: The Experience of Constructive Unionism, 1880–1905* (Cork University Press, 1987).

T. Garvin, *Nationalist Revolutionaries in Ireland, 1858–1922* (Clarendon Press, 1987).

K. Jeffery, *Ireland and the Great War* (Cambridge University Press, 2000).

M. Laffan, *The Partition of Ireland, 1911–25* (Dublin Historical Association, 1983).

M. Laffan, *The Resurrection of Ireland: The Sinn Féin Party, 1916–1921* (Cambridge University Press, 1999).

P. Maume, *The Long Gestation: Irish Nationalist Life, 1891–1918* (Gill and Macmillan, 1999).

Women in Ireland

M. E. Daly, *Women and Work in Ireland* (Economic and Social History Society of Ireland, 1997).

Y. Galligan, *Women and Politics in Contemporary Ireland: From the Margins to the Mainstream* (Pinter, 1998).

C. Murphy, *The Women's Suffrage Movement and Irish Society in the Early Twentieth Century* (Harvester Wheatsheaf, 1989).

D. Urquhart, *Women in Ulster Politics, 1890–1940* (Irish Academic Press, 2000).

M. G. Valiulis and M. O'Dowd (eds.), *Women and Irish History* (Wolfhound Press, 1997).

M. Ward, *Unmanageable Revolutionaries: Women and Irish Nationalism* (Pluto Press, 1995).

Cultural nationalism

R. F. Foster, *W. B. Yeats, a Life: The Apprentice Mage* (Oxford University Press, 1997).

J. Hutchinson, *The Dynamics of Cultural Nationalism: The Gaelic Revival and the Creation of the Irish Nation State* (Allen and Unwin, 1987).

F. S. L. Lyons, *Culture and Anarchy in Ireland, 1890–1939* (Oxford University Press, 1979, 1982).

Ireland since 1922

R. Fanning, *Independent Ireland* (Helicon, 1983).

T. Garvin, *1922: The Birth of Irish Democracy* (Gill and Macmillan, 1996).

P. Hart, *The IRA and its Enemies: Violence and Community in Cork, 1916–23* (Clarendon Press, 1998).

G. Hussey, *Ireland Today* (Viking, 1994).

A. Mitchell, *Revolutionary Government in Ireland: Dail Eireann, 1919–1922* (Gill and Macmillan, 1995).

E. O'Halpin, *The Decline of the Union: British Government in Ireland, 1892–1920* (Gill and Macmillan and Syracuse University Press, 1987).

J. Prager, *Building Democracy in Ireland* (Cambridge University Press, 1986).

J. M. Regan, *The Irish Counter-Revolution, 1921–1936* (Gill and Macmillan, 1999).

J. Whyte, *Church and State in Modern Ireland, 1823–1979* (Gill and Macmillan, 1980).

Northern Ireland

P. Bew, P. Gibbon, and H. Patterson, *Northern Ireland, 1921–1994: Political Forces and Social Classes* (Serif, 1995).

S. Bruce, *The Red Hand: Protestant Paramilitaries in Northern Ireland* (Oxford University Press, 1992).

P. Buckland, *The Factory of Grievances: Devolved Government in Northern Ireland, 1921–39* (Gill and Macmillan, 1979).

J. Loughlin, *The Ulster Question since 1945* (Macmillan, 1998).

J. McGarry and B. O'Leary, *Explaining Northern Ireland* (Blackwell, 1995).

M. Mulholland, *The Longest War: Northern Ireland's Troubled History* (Oxford University Press, 2002).

E. Phoenix, *Northern Nationalism: Nationalist Politics, Partition and the Catholic Minority in Northern Ireland, 1890–1940* (Ulster Historical Foundation, 1994).

R. Rose, *Governing Without Consensus: An Irish Perspective* (Faber and Faber, 1971).

J. Whyte, 'How much discrimination was there under the Unionist regime, 1921–68', in *Contemporary Irish Studies*, ed. T. Gallagher and J. O'Connell (Manchester University Press, 1983).

J. Whyte, *Interpreting Northern Ireland* (Clarendon Press, 1990).

Index

O

P

Index

Expand your collection of
VERY SHORT INTRODUCTIONS

Visit the
VERY SHORT INTRODUCTIONS
Web site

www.oup.co.uk/vsi

- ➤ **Information** about all published titles

- ➤ News of **forthcoming books**

- ➤ **Extracts** from the books, including titles not yet published

- ➤ **Reviews** and views

- ➤ **Links** to other **web sites** and main OUP web page

- ➤ Information about **VSIs in translation**

- ➤ **Contact** the editors

- ➤ **Order** other **VSIs** on-line

HISTORY
A Very Short Introduction
John H. Arnold

History: A Very Short Introduction is a stimulating
essay about how we understand the past. The book
explores various questions provoked by our understanding of history, and examines how these questions have
been answered in the past. Using examples of how historians work, the book shares the sense of excitement at
discovering not only the past, but also ourselves.

'A stimulating and provocative introduction to one of collective humanity's most important quests – understanding the past and its relation to the present. A vivid mix
of telling examples and clear cut analysis.'

David Lowenthal, University College London

'This is an extremely engaging book, lively, enthusiastic
and highly readable, which presents some of the fundamental problems of historical writing in a lucid and
accessible manner. As an invitation to the study of
history it should be difficult to resist.'

Peter Burke, Emmanuel College, Cambridge

www.oup.co.uk/vsi/history

ONLINE CATALOGUE
A Very Short Introduction

Our online catalogue is designed to make it easy to find your ideal Very Short Introduction. View the entire collection by subject area, watch author videos, read sample chapters, and download reading guides.

http://fds.oup.com/www.oup.co.uk/general/vsi/index.html

SOCIAL MEDIA
Very Short Introduction

Join our community

www.oup.com/vsi

- Join us online at the official Very Short Introductions **Facebook** page.
- Access the thoughts and musings of our authors with our online **blog**.
- Sign up for our monthly **e-newsletter** to receive information on all new titles publishing that month.
- Browse the full range of Very Short Introductions online.
- Read **extracts** from the Introductions for free.
- Visit our library of **Reading Guides**. These guides, written by our expert authors will help you to question again, why you think what you think.
- If you are a teacher or lecturer you can order inspection copies quickly and simply via our website.